TWENTY-SIX YEARS ON BARDSEY

Alexander John Loway

B. Sc., M. Phil

6ᵗʰ July 1996

Twenty-six Years on Bardsey

Bessie Williams
(translated from Welsh by Rosemary Gaches).

© *Bessie Williams 1996*

All rights reserved. No part of this publication may be reproduced or transmitted, in any form or by any means, without permission.

ISBN: 0-86381-350-X

First published in Welsh in 1992.

Printed in Wales by Gwasg Carreg Gwalch, 12 Iard yr Orsaf, Llanrwst, Gwynedd.

☎ *(01492) 642031*

A word to the reader

My mother has always been known as Nell Carreg throughout the Llŷn peninsula, since she spent 26 years of her life on Carreg Farm, Bardsey Island (*Ynys Enlli*, in Welsh). For a long time I, Bessie her daughter, have tried to chronicle and put together what she told me of her life there. This was written and published in Welsh.

I am very much indebted to Mrs Rosemary Gaches who translated this work so expertly, incorporating a few changes I suggested. Her work is a revised version of passages translated from my original Welsh book by six members of her Leighton Buzzard Welsh evening class, namely Ann Clancy, John Emlyn-Jones, David Griffiths, Stephen Harris, Joan Schneider and Marie Tippins. They enjoyed reading about life on Bardsey and were keen for others to share their enjoyment.

Bessie Williams

Part I

CHILDHOOD

I was born on the 17th of April 1905 in a little whitewashed cottage in the shadow of Y Foel, above Aberdaron on the tip of the Llŷn Peninsula. It's more than likely that the cottage, Talcen y Foel, was named after the hill. It was a small three-roomed house, with living-room, bedroom and loft. At one end was a cowshed, where one or two cows were kept. Even though the house was so small, it was quite cosy, as it was in the shelter of the hill and of the mountain, Mynydd Anelog.

Looking out from the door of the cottage, you could see most of the Uwchmynydd area, with Mynydd Mawr to the right, Ynysoedd y Gwylanod to the left, and Mynydd Enlli in the middle, rising from the sea as if it were guarding the Llŷn coast.

I was born one of five children — three sons and two daughters. There wasn't really enough room in the cottage to bring up a family of that size, but in spite of that we didn't come to any harm. Our old home was built more than two hundred years ago, and it is still in a reasonably good state, although no-one has lived in it for some years now.

My mother was brought up in Talcen y Foel by my grandparents and they had lived there since the time they were married. I remember very little of my oldest brother, for the lure of the sea called him away to sail the oceans. At the beginning of this century many young men from this district chose that life, perhaps for two reasons — to earn more money, for at that time it was difficult for farmers to keep their sons at home working on the farms, or because they thought it romantic to wander the length and breadth of the world.

After my brother had set off on a voyage, which sometimes lasted for months, after he'd wandered to and fro on his sailing-ship, and landed at many harbours all over the world, when the message came that his ship was coming back to this country, I was so excited I couldn't wait for him to get back. Longing to see him was the main reason for my excitement, but we couldn't help wondering what presents there would be for us. Of course, at that time, we children didn't get lots of presents like children do today. Most families couldn't afford presents even for birthdays or Christmas.

Although things were scarce Danial, Tomos and I were very happy. My sister Meri was younger. We children played with toys made out of old clothes, like rag dolls. We stitched rags together and stuffed them with hay or straw, making a ball to kick about. In spite of the poor toys we managed to enjoy ourselves.

My favourite plaything around the house was the little cat; she was my best friend. I tried to teach her tricks, and for her part she always wanted to be with me. But in spite of all the practice she was very slow to learn. She wouldn't do anything except for making sure that she had plenty of cuddles, and coming to the bedroom to sleep at night in a little box. I only had to say 'Go to sleep, Pussy' and she'd hop into the little box, I'd put a little cloth over her and she'd sleep in her little corner till the morning.

One of my mother's tasks each day was to milk the cow in the cowshed. One night, and it was a real cold winter's night, Mam had gone off to do the milking, and we children stayed in the house by the fire, as we did every night in winter. Some time after our chattering had died down, Tomos suddenly said, 'It would be nice to have a smoke'.

Of course we didn't have any tobacco at all to smoke, so Tomos got a bit of brown paper and rolled it up to make it look something like a cigarette. Then he stuck one end of it into the fire, and when it had started to burn, he drew the smoke into his mouth through the other end. When I saw that it worked, I tried to do the same, but it gave me a fright when the paper burst into flames in my hand and burned my face. Up I jumped in a great hurry and ran to the cowshed, calling out 'MAM', and she interrupted the milking and came out to see what was the matter.

The wind had made the burn worse. For about a fortnight after this mishap I had to take my food with the help of a teapot. The scar remains on my face to this day, and every time I look in the mirror the sight of the scar brings the incident back to life. As a result of this accident I have never smoked, throughout my life. The old folk in Llŷn say that a worthwhile lesson costs a lot. I'm sure that in every age children have intended to do as I did, but nowadays the temptation to smoke has turned into a habit for many young people in these parts.

I have very few memories of my childhood in our home at Talcen y Foel, as I wasn't very old when we lived there. The next thing that I remember was the news that we as a family were to turn our backs on our cottage, snuggling under The Foel, and that we were moving to live somewhere else. I didn't like the idea at all. After all, I was the little lass of Talcen y Foel, wasn't I? I was only a little girl of five, and my sister was hardly more than a baby.

The idea of moving to live somewhere else didn't appeal to me at all and I didn't know what it was going to involve either. This weighed on my mind for several days, and all I could do was think about where we were going to live.

My father was the owner of a boat, and when the regatta was held at Aberdaron each year, great were the preparations. He spent hours sorting out the sails, cleaning the boat and going over it with coaltar. My father could sail the boat just like someone driving a car today. He understood all the weather signs perfectly, and recognised all the tricks of the sea along the coastline, summer and winter.

My father won many prizes in his lifetime of sailing and we still have the cups today to prove what a good sailor he was along Aberdaron Bay. Perhaps it was the salt water in his veins which helped him to decide where we should move to, and that's when he told us we were going to live on Bardsey.

Even though we could see Bardsey Mountain clearly, I didn't know what life would be like on Bardsey Island. After a few weeks had gone by, the day came for us to move from the cottage and arrangements had to be made to borrow a horse and cart to come and fetch the furniture. The path to the cottage was nothing like the M1, so it was important to make the load secure, in case it worked loose in the cart and got smashed. Of course it wasn't possible to move all the furniture in one load, so the cart had to come back again and repeat the operation. When everything had been loaded, we went round the house and all the outbuildings to make sure we'd loaded all the tools.

Even though we were all ready to go to our new home, I wasn't at all happy about going to the house over the water. But my mother told me there was no need for me to make the journey, as the new people who were coming to live in Talcen y Foel would be very happy to look after me. To make things worse, I was given to understand that Pussy couldn't come with us. These words made me run crying to the cowshed, to try and hide there. No-one was going to take Pussy from me! After all the fuss, I finally won the argument and won a reprieve for Pussy on that occasion.

Although we were ready to set off from Talcen y Foel very early, the new family had arrived at the crack of dawn, with their furniture, and I remember how they brought into the house a dresser full of traditional blue dishes, such as you see nowadays in many houses in these parts. The dishes were shining like glass and they were all set out very neatly. Even today in my imagination I can see that dresser reflecting the sunlight which gave a lustre to it all.

When we'd finished loading up all the furniture and equipment, and had gone through the ceremony of checking through the sheds for everything of value, off we went, the whole family, to walk down to the village of Aberdaron. Arrangements had been made with the people of Bardsey as to what time they could expect us in Aberdaron.

ACROSS THE SOUND

We had all arrived at the village in plenty of time, but we had to wait for the boat to come across to take us to the island. There was no shortage of people on the beach to look out for the boat and, when it had landed, to help in loading it with the furniture and tools. The boat wasn't big enough to take everything in one load, but had to come back more than once to carry it all to safe harbour in Bardsey Anchorage (*Y Cafn*, in Welsh), where there was an ideal landing-place.

On the island for many days people had been asking questions and trying to imagine who would be the new tenants coming to live on the island.

'Where are they coming from?'
'Are they young people or old?'
'Have they got children?'

This guesswork was still going on on the island, when the boat reached Aberdaron to carry all our things over safely to our new home.

After loading the first load, they turned the bow of the boat ready for crossing the Sound. We set off with strong men plying the oars with their brawny arms. The boat moved slowly to start with, but began to move faster and more easily with the thrust of the oars. It seems that Pussy was the only one who crossed the water that day without seeing the sea at all, as she was hiding under my coat and sleeping soundly. After some hours had passed, or so it seemed at any rate, we came fairly close to the island. We'd almost crossed the Sound. Soon Pen Cristin came into sight and after we'd rounded the headland, the Anchorage came into view. Above the Anchorage, a large crowd of the island's inhabitants was waiting, gazing at us, and following the course of the boat into the safe harbour. I wasn't very interested in this sea voyage. The two hours that the boat had taken to travel gracefully across seemed like a whole day to me.

When we reached the Anchorage, we met the many inhabitants who had assembled to welcome us to our new home. After shaking hands and listening to their many words of welcome, we began to go up into the island, along the only road, the one which runs from the Anchorage to the houses.

ARRIVING AT CARREG

Our journey along the rocky road was interrupted by someone saying, 'Those two houses there are Tŷ Pella and Rhedynog Goch, and that's the lime kiln.'

Then as we paused for a moment to look at the building, someone else broke into the conversation, pointing at a building which was coming into view and saying,

'That's the school, or as some say, the old chapel.'

'Where's Carreg Fawr?'

'Oh, you've got to walk a little further yet, past two houses, Cristin and Cristin Isaf, and then across the road is Plas Bach.'

By now my legs felt as if they would collapse under me but in spite of this, I carried on trying to keep up with everyone else walking along the road.

After we had gone a little further, somebody said, 'There's Carreg Fawr', and we all stopped to look at the building, which was a field's width from the road. It was lovely to walk on the grass, after walking so much on the uneven road.

Down we went to the farmhouse. It was a palace compared with Talcen y Foel.

Goodness gracious, it was the loveliest mansion I had ever seen, with big, clear windows reaching right up into the sky. My goodness, I'd never seen anything like it!

When I went into the house, there was plenty of room for me to run about from one room to another. It was a bit of a change to move from a small, ordinary two-chimney cottage, with its three rooms, to a house with four bedrooms, two living rooms, kitchen and buttery, as they called the room which was used for cooking food.

I was enjoying myself, running from one room to another, but soon I had to stop running around, as I kept getting in the way of the men who were bringing the furniture from the cart into the house, and putting everything in its proper place. By the time they had finished, the evening had flown past, and I had to go to bed straightaway.

Part II

BUILDINGS — THE MONUMENT

After a good night's sleep, the newcomers got up the following morning, even though they had been tired out after the hard work of the previous day. In no time breakfast was ready in our new house. We hurried through our food that morning so that we could do a tour of the island and see its marvels.

We had seen five houses before reaching Carreg; now we set off again along the road and came to Tŷ Bach and Tŷ Nesaf, two of the other farms. Then an old ruin came into view, and the chapel and Tŷ Capel, and at the end of the road came the last two farms, namely Nant and Hen Dŷ. From there we could see the Mainland. That is the name the Bardsey islanders have given to the Llŷn Peninsula. Pointing to the mainland, one of the islanders said to Mam,

'Do you see that furthest mountain over yonder? That's where Talcen y Foel is.'

I tried to make out where it was, but I couldn't see it at all, although I tried as best I could.

I've mentioned the ten farms there were on the island, and all the buildings were lovely to look at. Indeed the sheds for the animals looked much better than many of the houses on the mainland — not surprising since the farms dated from 1875.

And what about the cottages? There was one which to this day remains in excellent condition, a small one-chimney cottage, a bit like Talcen y Foel, nestling at the foot of the mountain, and facing towards the southern side of the island. Carreg Bach was the name of that pretty little cottage which reminded me of my old home.

Looking over the wall next to the chapel, I saw two beautiful monuments in the graveyard, and I asked my companion in whose memory the monuments had been erected.

'Well, I can tell you right away,' he answered. 'Do you see the smaller one of the two?'

'Yes,' I said.

'Lord Newborough, the owner of the island, took a great interest in the islanders and their circumstances. It was he who built the houses which are now on the island. All of them were finished in the year 1875. That's the monument Lord Newborough raised to commemorate the twenty thousand saints who are buried on the island. When you get a chance, go and look at the unusual inscriptions on it.'

'And what of the other monument?'

'Oh, that's the monument erected after his death. It cost a lot of money and was very heavy, and they had a lot of trouble getting it to the island, or so rumour has it.'

The monument to the saints stands nine feet tall and is inscribed on three sides, on the first side in Latin.

> In hoc loco requiescant.

The second inscription says:

> Respect the remains of 20,000 saints buried near this spot.

On the third side is the following verse:

> Safe is this island
> Where each saint would be.
> How wilt thou smile
> Upon life's stormy sea?

CHOOSING A KING — THE GREAT EXODUS

In the sixties Lord Newborough gave the tenants the right to choose someone from among themselves to be king. John Williams was chosen to govern the island and a ceremony was held to crown the king. He was given a crown, a cross and an army. His reign did not last long. He was deposed and died in the poorhouse in Pwllheli.

Love Pritchard was chosen to take his place. *Y Genedl* (The Nation) gives the following statistics for the year of 1921, showing that the king had a large number of subjects under his rule. The population consisted of 58 people — 34 men and 24 women. There were 11 families. 8 persons spoke only English, 11 spoke only Welsh, 28 were bilingual and there were 5 children.

In 1924 there were 48 cattle, 21 horses, several score of sheep, some dozens of pigs and chickens, a few ducks; 16 cats and 12 dogs. The population numbered 71, 36 male and 35 female.

I've already mentioned people leaving the island, and now I'd like to mention what happened in the great exodus which was soon to happen. The decision was made to leave the island because the problems of crossing between the island and the mainland were becoming more difficult all the time. Also the young people were leaving, and they were the ones who were skilled with the boats and understood all about the tides; the rest had reached a fair age and found it difficult to cross to Aberdaron to fetch goods and food.

Moving away from the island was very painful. It was especially hard for the oldest inhabitants to leave their old homes. A meeting of the islanders was called to consider the matter seriously and they decided that it was impossible to carry on, and that the best thing would be to leave.

In conversation with a reporter from *Y Genedl* one of the inhabitants expressed surprise that the government hadn't given cable or wireless to the island to connect it with the mainland. I remember a doctor being called to the island. He started back at five o'clock in the evening and it was three o'clock in the morning when he reached Aberdaron. He said it was the last time he would go to Bardsey, even if everyone there was ill.

Only a few blocks of stone remain today from the old abbey. Many of the stones were used to build the present chapel. The chapel was the meeting place for the islanders. There too the literary meetings and such like were held, as well as services on Sundays and on important festivals during the year.

THE LIGHTHOUSE

There is another splendid building on the island, built of stone from Anglesey. This building is the lighthouse. It doesn't stand on its own; alongside it are houses for the men who looked after the lighthouse machinery.

This building was designed by a man called Joseph Nielson, and he was also responsible for seeing the work was done according to his instructions. It took quite a time to complete the building. It was finished in 1821 or 1822.

According to the plan, as well as the lighthouse, a foghorn had to be built. This very important instrument made a deafening sound whenever thick fog came down and hid the dangerous rocks of Bardsey from passing ships.

The power of the light in a lighthouse was measured in candles at that time, and the power of the Bardsey light was 270,000. The light enabled many a ship to work out its position pretty accurately. Then the ship would continue its journey to the harbour it was making for. The purpose of the foghorn was to warn that danger was near and its noisy message alerted ships to keep their distance.

When the lighthouse was built, houses were also built there, so that the men who looked after the machinery could live comfortably. In turn their wives and children came there for a while, and we children were glad to have someone new to play with, and of course we got the opportunity to teach Welsh to the children.

One thing which was especially enjoyable to us children was being allowed to go into the lighthouse and walk up the 250 steps to the mirrors which reflected the light at night. The mirrors in the lighthouse were specially made to transmit the flashes in the night.

After we had climbed up all the steps we could see the handle being turned to raise the weights from the bottom. The weights turned the lantern, thus producing the flashes. This had to be done every two hours through the night or the light would stay in one place, and that would be dangerous to ships as there would be nothing to show how many flashes there were meant to be. Every lighthouse is known by its flashes, the number of flashes and the frequency.

When the fog was thick, the men had to start the engine which filled the air tanks and released the air at regular intervals to sound the foghorn. If you sat under this noisy instrument, the awful din had a serious effect on your hearing, and it was fun coming from there unable to hear anyone talking for a long time.

Three men looked after the lighthouse until comparatively recently, and we'll talk about some of them later on.

Part III

OLD BUILDINGS

There is one building I have not mentioned yet, and that is the storehouse, which I'm sure is a much older building than the others. All the islanders who went out fishing used to keep their fishing equipment in it, and that is still its purpose today.

These are some of the old cottages that were on the island before we arrived there: there were two cottages near the school, one used by the smugglers as a public house, and the other a private dwelling. In the field below Tŷ Bach was an old cottage called Dalar.

Between the Anchorage and the lighthouse stood a cottage called Penrhyn. Then on the other side of the lighthouse were the old ruined walls of Pen Diben, where the islanders used to drive the sheep when they needed to be checked. At the northern tip of the island was Penrhyn Gogar cottage. Some traces of it remain to this day.

PLAYING

As children we would pretend that the old walls of Pen Fron were our little house. This was a sufficiently safe place for us to play without anyone having to look after us.

Although Sam and I were the only children on the island, fairly soon a family with young children arrived. I was delighted to have friends to play with.

There weren't enough children to make a team for playing

games, but we girls would look for pieces of crockery to play house, and pretend to make tea and then pour it into some fragment of a cup. We would use leaves of different shapes to make biscuits and cakes, and sometimes make some with mud and water.

I remember once running home from where we were playing house in a quiet corner at the foot of the mountain, to fetch a little water. Passing near the mountain wall I saw a man and a lady on the ground and the man was strangling the lady. I shouted for my father and he came as fast as he could to see what was the matter.

'Come at once, there is a man killing a lady.'

He hurried back with me, but of course as soon as we arrived there, he realised what was going on and gave me a telling off for fetching him on such a pretext. How was I to know what was going on?

There wasn't time for us to play lots of games. For one thing, there was work to do on the farm, or the boat would have been to Aberdaron and we had to lend a hand to carry all the provisions from the Anchorage. But we had time to play draughts or ludo. A few of us could play these games. Mrs McCowen of Carreg Plas, Aberdaron was very generous to the children of the island, and she gave us one good game.

She purchased a huge picture of a donkey to put on the wall. Then the children would put a blindfold on their faces and try to put the donkey's tail in the right place. Sometimes someone would put it in a most unlikely place and we had a great deal of fun playing with the donkey's tail.

The lads used to enjoy themselves with a ferret and go across the fields or the mountainside searching for rabbits, keeping the live ones until the boat took them across. This wasn't just play as it was profitable work too.

THE ISLANDERS

It isn't easy today to remember how all the islanders were related to each other, but I can remember the people who were living in the houses when I came to the island.

One really interesting fact was that there was not one married couple on the island, only bachelors and spinsters and one lame child called Sam. I don't know who his mother and father were.

Now I will try to list all the population of the island without putting Mr or Miss in front of their names. This was the custom at that time, to call everyone by their Christian name, followed by the name of their house.

In Tŷ Capel lived a young minister. I believe that his name was Rev. R. Evans but I'm not sure. There were two farms, Nant and Hen Dŷ, farmed by William and his uncle Robat. Robat was an old sailor who had retired and come home to help on the land. They must have been fairly rich to keep a maid the whole year, and the maid was remarkably competent in all her tasks.

I'll turn next to Tŷ Bach, where there lived two sisters and a brother, namely Siân, Meri and Siôn. It was evident that that they weren't short of a penny in Tŷ Bach, and I heard a rumour that Siân had discovered a purse full of money by the seaside. Everyone thought the story was true, because of the look of the house.

In Tŷ Nesaf there was a lame boy who lived with three uncles, Ifan, Tomos and Dei. No-one was sure who his mother was, but I think she was Catherine Ann. There was also a maid in this farm all the time and I remember three different maids there, namely Jane, Ann Roberts Tŷ'n Mynydd Anelog, and Lora. In Carreg Bach, the old cottage originally built with a thatched roof but now with a roof of slates, lived Tomos and his sister Siân.

In Plas Bach, one of the biggest farms on the island, lived Captain John Williams. He had to give up sailing the high seas because he broke his leg. Since there was no doctor on board ship at the time, the leg had to get better by itself. Unfortunately it became completely twisted and he could no longer carry on his job. He was a cheerful character, but while at the farm on Bardsey he couldn't move around very much. Still he was a likeable character, full of wit, and interesting company.

What he enjoyed most was getting a few people to listen to his memories of events at sea. I'm sure that these stories of his inspired many others to go to sea and travel to those parts described by Captain Williams.

He had set up his home in Plas Bach with his niece. She was married but very little was seen of her husband, since his mother was ill and infirm, and he had to spend his time looking after her. That was why he didn't come to Bardsey. The Captain had two farmhands to work at Plas Bach, one of whom was a very impulsive and irritable fellow. One night my father thought he would have a bit of fun with this character. He got up at about three o'clock in the morning and went to call on the lad for help. He told him that the cow couldn't throw her calf. The fellow got up at once and went running off only half-dressed and without doing up his bootlaces. When he reached the cowshed he asked in a panic,

'Where's the cow, Robat?'

'Well, well,' said my father, 'have you forgotten what day it is today? It's April Fool's Day.'

The farmhand was hopping mad when he heard this and he said under his breath, 'April Fool be damned! I'd kill you, but I don't want to have everyone talking about me. You blithering idiot!'

Somehow my father wasn't happy that he'd played such a dirty trick on him, so he never breathed a word about the incident.

Almost across the road from Plas Bach is Cristin farm where three very odd characters used to live. They were two brothers and a sister, and the two brothers, Wil and Harri, were a stubborn pair. Their sister Siân had a very hard time of it with the two of them. The two would never have the same thing for dinner or supper. One wanted tatws llaeth (*potatoes in buttermilk*) and the other wanted llymru (*flummery*). One wanted brwas and the other wanted llymru. It wasn't an easy task making brwas and llymru. In case any of my readers do not know how to prepare these dishes, here are the recipes for both so that you can see the trouble the sister used to have with the two brothers.

First the brwas. Place some bread in the bottom of the bowl, adding a little salt and some hot water. Place the oat bread on top, but don't make it too thick. Pour melted dripping over it all and leave it to soak through. Then add more oat bread and leave it to soak for three days. Then strain it well, place the liquid in a saucepan and boil it well until it has thickened. Then take it out and place it in a clean dish and leave it to stand until it has set well, then eat it with milk.

The llymru. Take a pint of buttermilk and a pound of oatmeal and leave the mixture to soak for three days. Then strain it well. Then place the liquid in a saucepan and boil it well until it has thickened. Then take it out and place it in a clean dish and leave it to stand until it has set well; then eat it with milk.

I wonder if the two brothers realised how much trouble they caused their sister?

One day the sister had an accident and broke her arm. One of the brothers took her to the doctor in Aberdaron, but what he said to the doctor was,

'There's no point spending too much on her, she's getting pretty old.'

Neither Siân nor Wil had been away from the island onto the mainland very much. But one day Wil decided he would go as far as Fourcrosses (now called Y Ffôr) near Pwllheli. On the journey there he saw many strange and wonderful sights and he was amazed that the world was so big.

'Good Heavens, I didn't think this old world was as big as that,' he said. Wil was exceedingly fond of nature, and didn't even like to see anyone kill a bluebottle eager to leave its mark on fresh meat.

In Rhedynog Goch (which the people of Bardsey abbreviated to Dyno Goch) lived a brother and sister called Huw and Margiad, if I remember correctly. They were the only two on the island who didn't attend chapel. The main reason for this was that the two couldn't get about very well, because of rheumatism more than likely, and also it was quite a step from Dyno Goch to the chapel.

I don't know what the two lived on. They couldn't farm or do anything else to bring in money. There must have been money there somewhere but I never heard anyone talking about it. Of course there was no such thing as Social Security in those days.

Many people have asked me, 'How did Tŷ Pella (*Furthest House*) get its name when it's the nearest house to the landing stage?' The reason of course is that Tŷ Pella is one of the houses furthest from the Monastery. Tŷ Pella was the home of the king at that time.

Part IV

THE KING

The King was a lazy old creature, ready to put his head down anywhere, but he was especially fond of going to sleep on his settle when he was at home. He would sleep for several hours at a time, especially after dinner. He must have heard the English saying, 'After dinner sleep a while', without hearing the whole couplet, 'After supper walk a mile'.

When I was a child, I used to go and work there during the day. I didn't go there out of choice. One task I had to perform every day was doing up his bootlaces. The old boy was too lazy to do that. But he wasn't too lazy to chew shag tobacco. The tobacco he used was of the strongest kind. There was another ceremony connected with his tobacco-chewing. He had to get rid of the lump of tobacco from his mouth, and he needed a spittoon to spit into. The thing I hated most was cleaning this disgusting implement.

He lived with his sister and his niece. There was also a man called Tomos there, but I don't know whether the two of them were related or not. Like many of the young girls on the island, the niece was very capable, and always ready to take part in the chapel services, and like all the intelligent girls, she tried her best to teach us children. I never had a day of schooling, and spent only a little time in Sunday School.

This girl had a friend called Mr Siccum; he was said to be gentry. But we children thought he was her sweetheart, for the reason that every time he came to Bardsey on the lighthouse ship, the two spent many hours in the dairy! It's quite certain they didn't go there to do the churning! But I never had enough courage to go and peep through the door or the keyhole, although I was dying to have a look.

When this gentleman came to Bardsey, he would bring her lots of clothes — of the latest fashion — and they looked quite splendid on her. He would also bring her some items for the house. It was much more beautiful than any other house on the island. But we didn't dare say anything to anyone about the king's house.

Farmhands and girls used to come to Bardsey from the mainland to work on the farms or as housemaids. A man called Owen Ffatri of Pen-y-Caerau near Aberdaron would recruit young men and girls to work on the island, and he was also responsible for fixing their wages.

Owen Ffatri was connected with Bardsey because he had married someone called Sydna, who lived on the island. Normally about four people were employed on Bardsey. It wasn't the thought of young girls or anything like that that persuaded the men to go to the island but rather the hope of getting paid and saving a little money during their stay on the island.

THE CARPENTER — CLOTHES

Since the houses on the island had been recently built, there was not a great deal of need for painting and papering. From time to time a certain amount had to be done to keep the place looking bright and neat.

We were fortunate that John Thomas the carpenter lived on the island, spending his time repairing boats and also building them if there was need. Anyone who wanted some painting or papering done only had to call at John's home, Carreg Bach, and he would come and see what was needed. The housewife didn't have to go to the mainland to choose the paper. John would go and buy the paper and hang it on the wall. But in Carreg he happened to hang one piece of paper upside down, and so it stayed, but no-one noticed it since it was behind the door.

If painting was needed, it was John who got some idea of the required colour and went across to the mainland to fetch the paint, and that was the painting problem solved.

John Thomas of Carreg Bach was very fond of children and spent a lot of his time amusing them and playing with them. He came to Carreg one day and he was extremely tired. Although he was tired, Wil kept trying to persuade him to play, but John said, 'Don't, lad, I'm feeling really poorly', and he closed his eyes to try and get five minutes or so of sleep. Wil went and fetched a thin stick, rapped poor old John across the knuckles and said to him, 'Mustn't poorly, dammit'.

The women of Plas ym Mhenllech used to buy underclothes from William Evans, who kept a shop in Aberdaron, but as a rule the women of Bardsey would send for clothes from catalogues like J.D. Williams and Oxendale. If you turn to page 9 or 10 of the J.D. Williams catalogue for 1899 you will see that there were plenty of frocks for children for two shillings and a woman's frock for seven and sixpence.

Most of the men would be too shy to go to the shop in Aberdaron to buy underwear for the women. After they returned to Bardsey they took delight in seeing the women wearing their new clothes.

FOOD

I can imagine someone asking, 'What did you eat on the island?'

This was the pattern of our meals. In the morning we would have porridge made from oatmeal or sometimes brwas for breakfast. Then after the porridge or brwas, a slice of home-made bread with butter and treacle on it.

Then for dinner, potatoes and meat or fish fresh from the sea, fried or roasted. We didn't have much for tea in the afternoon, just a cup of something to keep us going till supper. Then for supper we had eggs and a big slice of bacon from a pig fattened on the island. People used to salt the bacon and hang it from the ceiling and cut slices as and when they needed them.

If anyone wanted a change, it was easy to get a rabbit for dinner or supper. All we had to do was to go out to the fields with a ferret and send it down a rabbit-hole. In no time at all we would hear a great commotion down in the bowels of the earth and then the rabbit would shoot out as if fired by a gun and the dog would catch it in a twinkling. Once we'd caught the rabbit, we would skin it, clean it and stuff it with sage and onion.

There were often times when flour became scarce and so, as there was no bread available, there was nothing for it but to search out a sheaf of oats. Then people would use a flail, made of two sticks, such as was used in days gone by, to free the ears from the stalk. It is not easy work for anyone today to use the flail. It was an advantage to have the wind blowing from a particular direction, so that we could open the two doors of the building where the flailing was going on and the chaff would get blown out.

Ten minute turns for everyone was the custom with threshing because it was heavy work. At the end of all the toil, the product would be worth having because it made wonderful flour for unleavened bread baked on a hot griddle.

If the food shortage continued, the lighthouse men would come to the rescue because they had more than enough food to last for over two months, the time they would be on the island. It was not easy for the islanders on Bardsey to buy enough flour to last for many months because not many of the households had money to spare.

The lighthousemen's flour was sealed in large tins and because of this, kept in a specially good condition for a long time.

Every Saturday morning Mam would bake bread. When she had prepared it all and put it in a warm place for the yeast to raise the dough, I would look forward to getting a large slice of home-baked bread with plenty of butter on it. At suppertime we could also roast potatoes in the oven with plenty of bacon rashers on top, and to finish the meal Mam would make large dishes of rice pudding which would be full of cream. No, today's Ambrosia doesn't compare with that. Everyone would look forward to supper and we would eat more than was good for us. No-one ever mentioned slimming in those days.

TOBACCO AND COAL

When we had stormy weather, one of the first things to run out was tobacco. One man, a really elderly man, said to my father, 'I could live without food if I had enough tobacco.'

Once when we were without flour, the old fogey had to change his tune. It was no small matter to be without flour or a loaf of bread in the house.

'I'll never talk about tobacco again Robat, as long as there's a thick slice of home-baked bread for me.'

Almost all of the men smoked shag, the tobacco that was as black as coal. Hard tobacco was also available, and a lot of the men used to cut it with a sharp knife, rub it in their hands and smoke it in their pipes. When the weather was foul in the Sound, it wasn't easy to get across to refill the tobacco pouch.

When their tobacco ran out completely, there was nothing to do but collect coltsfoot leaves, and fortunately there were enough of these leaves to be had on the island.

Of course it was cold at times on the island, and in order to keep warm we had to have a good fire. We had to have coal. It wasn't practical in those days to go to Aberdaron to get coal, but there was an arrangement by which the islanders got a small boat to bring coal to Bardsey. As it was a small boat, it was easy for it to come into the Anchorage at high tide. After securing the boat there, the islanders would wait for some hours until the tide went out and left the boat on dry land. Then they would come down to the beach with horses and carts and back the carts up to the boat.

The boat had a winch on its mast, with a large bucket attached to the winch. After lowering this tub down into the hold of the boat, it was filled by the crew, then winched up again full of coal and unloaded into the carts. It was all very tiring work. Not only were the men tired but also the horses, from standing on the beach and being frightened every time the tub was emptied into the cart. Two very strong men were needed to hold the horses and stop them kicking up a fuss, and some of the coal was spilt on the beach.

I remember one time, when the small boat had come to Bardsey, and as usual had anchored to wait for the tide, a storm blew up and we had thunder and lightning. The crew couldn't do anything but stay on the boat waiting for the wind to abate. But in spite of all their waiting, the wind didn't drop, and they had to call the men from the lighthouse to come with rockets and strong ropes. A rocket with a thin rope attached was fired and arrived safely on board the little boat. Then it was easy to get a strong rope to the boat. After securing the ropes it wasn't long before the crew got safely ashore. But before long the little boat was hurled onto the sharp rocks and was broken up. The crew were in tears to see their boat being broken up by the storm and their livelihood at risk.

The next day the coal had been washed up onto the beach, but as it was a Sunday no-one even dared to think of collecting it. Although it was a Sunday, one old chap considered it a waste not to collect it all, and although some people tried to persuade him not to gather coal, he started the laborious task. Someone said to him,

'If you do that, you'll never walk properly again.'

And that's what happened, believe you me, he couldn't walk the next day or the day after, and the poor soul died three weeks later. And of course we children had a good excuse when someone asked us to do something on a Sunday.

TOYS

As I said earlier, when we were children we had to amuse ourselves because we hardly had any toys. Yet we did have some, thanks to my father's skill as a craftsman. He was very good with his hands. In our house, as in many in the area, there were pictures hanging on the wall. In Carreg we had one picture, a picture of John Elias of Anglesey, hanging on the kitchen wall where it could be seen every day. My mother loathed it, because his eyes seemed to follow every move she made. In the end it got taken down and stuffed behind the cupboard.

One rainy day my father retrieved the picture. He pulled off the cord that was used to hang it on the wall, and the back of the picture as well. Having got rid of these, John Elias was ready to leave his home. Freed from his imprisonment, poor John Elias was cremated. My father carefully removed the glass from the frame, looked for a decent piece of wood, and marked it in neat little squares, each one the same size. We children couldn't understand what he was doing. He painted the squares black and white. Then he cut down the frame with a saw and replaced the glass.

At this point we realised it was a draughts board. But how on earth was he going to get counters for us to play with? He went out and came back after a little while with a rake handle in his hand. He sawed the round stick into little blocks, then carved them carefully with a knife and painted them black and white. We couldn't wait for the paint to dry, but we had to wait or we would have messed up our hands and perhaps our clothes.

We all enjoyed playing on that board. I wonder where it is today? It was better made than the stuff you get today.

THE PLACE OF WORSHIP (CHAPEL AND SCHOOL)

I remember one Sunday when a minister came over to preach and got soaked to the skin while crossing to Bardsey. One of the family of Hendre Bach, Y Ffôr, gave him a good suit to change into out of the wet clothes. Unfortunately he took the suit back with him. No-one ever saw the suit nor the minister thereafter on Bardsey.

Once a month the minister would hold the service of the Sacrament of the Lord's Supper. John Thomas, Carreg Bach, had made a wonderful cupboard to keep the communion vessels in. It was made of oak wood and finished with wood stain. Perhaps that cupboard is in the chapel still, but I know that the communion vessels are in one of the museums in Wales.

When a minister decided to leave Bardsey, after accepting an invitation to some other church, for a while there would be no-one to watch over the church and that happened on Bardsey before Rev. Owen Jones agreed to come.

It was always a special day when a new minister came to live on the island. A crowd had assembled on the beach in the Anchorage to welcome the new minister and his family. After the boat had landed on the beach, there was a lot of work to do. We had to empty the boat of all the furniture and belongings and carry everything up to the chapel, the longest journey on the island. Amongst all the belongings there was one small bundle wrapped in a warm shawl and the Reverend took care of it. 'I will carry this,' he said, and so he did.

About three quarters of the way to the chapel the Reverend felt tired from carrying the bundle and he gave the bundle to his wife. After she'd taken the bundle she realised that her husband had carried the little boy upside down all along the road. Poor little Emrys, but he'd come to no harm.

Rev. Owen Jones was a very busy man when there was a service in the chapel. Because there was no-one apart from him who could play the organ in those days, he was up and down like a squirrel from pulpit to organ.

Although poor little Emrys had been carried upside down, he grew into a lively boy, walking and talking very young and needing someone with eyes in the back of their head to watch him all the time. He could always find some mischief to get into. When he was about two and a half years old I remember him running from his seat in the chapel to the pulpit, where his dad was in the middle of his sermon. 'Come down, Dad, so I can tell you something,' he said. Another time, with the congregation rising to sing, he said, 'Mam, Mam, I've done a weewee on the seat and it's flowing like a river down onto the floor.' But fair play to him, he cheered up many of the congregation, I'm sure.

As I told you before, I never had a single day's schooling, except at home, learning housework. I missed a great deal by not being able to go to school, as did many other children at that time. It's more than likely that there are children today who would be envious of us, since they are not interested in learning.

Fortunately there was the Sunday School, which gave me the opportunity to learn to read and write a certain amount, and also to learn a lot of things by heart. Sunday School was held in the chapel of course. There were normally three services on a Sunday, and reading sessions during the week. The minister would regularly hold a Bible study class on a weekday evening.

When Rev. J.W. Jones came as minister to Bardsey, he started a school for the children. Classes were held from five o'clock to six every evening when it could be arranged, without interfering with any other meeting which was due to take place.

One night my mother invited the minister to supper. There was nothing unusual about this. Many people would invite him around for a meal, and we were fairly sure where Mam would get him to sit at the table, that is on the settle.

When we had got the house to ourselves, we stuck a needle into the lid of the settle, with its pointed end sticking out. The time came for the minister to arrive and Mam offered him his place at the table. He moved towards it.

'Come and sit here on the settle.'

And now this poor, innocent creature goes and sits down on the exact spot where the needle is lying in wait. No sooner had he sat down than he jumped to his feet, shouting:

'Goodness gracious, what's that?'

When he'd got over the shock, he drew his hand across his trousers and saw blood on his hand. I can't remember whether he ate anything or not before going home. But I'm sure that the incident with the needle affected his gait that evening.

After the accident, my father made a close inspection of the settle and saw the needle sticking up through the slit.

'How on earth did that get there?' he asked.

In silence Mam turned to us two children and saw the guilt plainly written on our faces. She said nothing that evening but packed us off to bed without ceremony.

Believe me, we never played any tricks on Jôs the minister after that!

THE START OF THE WAR 1914

The years of my childhood passed by until in 1914 came the start of the First World War: that is a day I will never forget. The reason why I remember the date is that on that day my brother died on the boat on which he was working. He was only twenty-four. His funeral was in Liverpool and that is where he was buried. Our family didn't have enough money to pay for him to be brought home to Llŷn. This event affected my mother deeply and she was never the same again after losing him.

The war had little effect on the islanders on Bardsey and their daily routine. But there were some interesting events which we children remembered. It was fairly common for us to see a convoy (a number of ships) passing Bardsey with warships around them to protect them from the enemy. Enemy submarines used to watch out for them and wait for a chance to destroy the merchant ships which were virtually important to us in Britain.

I remember seeing several ships being sunk. The crews of some of the ships were told to get into the boats and land on Bardsey, where they would be safe, as they thought that Bardsey was a neutral island.

One fine Summer morning a small sailing ship was sailing fairly close to the island. Suddenly it sank. The crew came safely ashore onto the island.

None of them had time to collect any of their personal belongings. One was in bed when the ship sank and he came ashore without his trousers. But that wasn't what was worrying the lad. The accident happened on his twenty-first birthday. Before setting out on the voyage, about a week earlier, he had learned that his father had died. His greatest worry was how on earth he could let his mother know that he was alive and well on the island.

The crew were all Irish and that evening they entertained us by singing Irish songs to us. It was a concert to remember for all of us.

After they'd eaten well and warmed up by the fire, and when the concert was over, we all slept until the morning. When we'd got up and had breakfast, it was arranged that they would cross the Sound in one of the Bardsey boats. When they reached Aberdaron, the crew had to try to make their way home or to the port their ship had been making for.

One Saturday morning, when only my sister and I were in the

house, there was the sound of knocking on the door. In terror we ran from pillar to post, to see what was happening. We were terrified when we saw eleven men, wearing oilskins and wellingtons, and looking exhausted and unkempt. The two of us were frightened to death and we thought the end had come.

Mam appeared from somewhere and realised that they needed food. They were the crew of a British boat and they'd run out of food on the boat. Mam sold them a lot of butter, eggs, vegetables, fish and meat. The men were more than ready to buy anything that could be eaten.

Mam made a pretty penny selling her delicious food to them and they were very grateful for it. It was the biggest order she had whilst on the island.

Suddenly, one Saturday night, there was a shout from someone,

'Come quickly, the crew of a ship, two boats full of them, are trying to land in Porth Solfach.'

They were trying to land in a very dangerous part of the island, where there were sharp rocks underwater.

When they found out what the problem was, everyone legged it over to Porth Solfach. I arrived there with the crowd. After a considerable struggle, they got the boats ashore without mishap.

There were thirteen men in the boats and they seemed to be in a bad way, with dried seawater on their faces and all looking the worse for wear. They had been at sea in their boats for many days without food or drink, and some of them were almost fainting.

Initially everyone thought they were Germans and most of them only spoke one language, but the mate could speak a bit of English, and after trying to get some information out of him, we finally discovered that they were a crew from Norway. Having talked to them, we realised we had an enormous problem. What to do with them? Something needed to be done quickly, so the islanders held a sort of committee there and then. Whilst this was going on, the poor souls from Norway looked really worried, as they couldn't understand what was going on.

In the end the committee came to a decision. Since there were ten farms on the island, each farm would take one of the poor wretches. But the numbers didn't add up. There were three left over. They pleaded with the minister to take one, but he refused pointblank. From that moment on, for as long as he remained minister on the island, he was held in low esteem.

In the end the families at the three largest farms took two each and that solved the problem of accommodation. One of the crew was coming to stay with us. We set off homewards with the lodger and he seemed fit to drop. He was as weak as a child and desperate for something to eat.

On reaching the house, the first thing Mam did was to look for dry underclothes and my father's second best suit. When she'd got everything together, she led the stranger into the parlour for him to sort himself out. When he'd finished in the parlour, he joined us in the kitchen. In the meantime Mam had put the round table in front of a roaring fire. Before the starving man she put a plate of potatoes with plenty of tasty bacon, and a bowlful of rice pudding to follow. When he'd finished eating, Mam gave him a cup of tea. Although he begged for more food, Mam was wise enough not to give him any even though he was still famished. It's not wise to give too much food to a starving man — it could make things worse. Mam spent ages trying to make him understand that he couldn't have any more food for a while. Then with his fingers on the clock he tried to work out when he'd get his next meal.

He put his head on the table as if he were sulking, but that wasn't the reason. Mam pointed at the settle, suggesting that the man would be far warmer sleeping there than in bed upstairs.

There was a multi-coloured cushion on the settle, made from scraps of many colours and Mam gave him that as a pillow. Also there was a present she'd had from an aunt, Mrs Evans, Trem-y-Don, who lived in Pwllheli. The present was a homemade woollen blanket with a red border. This was truly the 'special' blanket, used by us children if we were unwell. Mam used to wrap us in the blanket until we were over our illness.

At this time there was an old ship's captain living on the island, a man who had retired after wandering the seas all his life. And it was the old captain who took in the mate. Of course, with a captain and a mate in conversation, there was talk of nothing but the sea. After talking for some hours, the mate realised that he knew the old captain.

When the captain was preparing to go on a voyage to Norway, the cabin boy who looked after him fell ill, and he had to get another cabin boy to sail with him. Before setting off, he got news of a boy from Norway who was eager to go to his native land and he gave the job to him.

After talking about his life at sea, the truth came out, namely that this was the lad who had been cabin boy to the old captain. I don't remember how long the crew from Norway were on the island but I well remember seeing a ship from the British navy coming to fetch them from the island.

It was a really sad day, with almost every one of the inhabitants standing on the beach saying farewell. Many a tear was shed by the islanders and the crew all realised, I'm sure, that they'd received a regal welcome on the island. Wouldn't it be interesting to know if any one of them is alive today? It would be interesting to meet and talk about the occasion. They had shelter and relief from the horror of war, if only temporarily.

Part V

DREAMS

Do you believe in dreams? Whether you do or not, this is what happened to my father one night. He dreamed that something valuable came ashore behind Bardsey Mountain. Although we tried to reason with him the next morning, we couldn't make him change his mind and he started striding off there before he'd had his breakfast and without milking the cows. I had to milk the cows that morning.

When he arrived there, indeed there were some tins, eight of them with some sort of powder in them. Either they had been hidden or they were where the tide had left them on the dry rocks. The authorities were advised about the tins and before long some men came from the authorities to collect the tins and paid my father a substantial amount of money for his work. There you are, one dream at least that came true.

ZEPPELINS

I have talked about some of the warships that were around the island. Sometimes they would throw bags of flour into the sea and then the fishermen would row over to fetch them and lift them into their boat. As the flour was finely ground, the salt water didn't do it much harm. Only about a penny thickness of the flour would have got wet and it was easy to separate the wet from the dry flour.

I remember well the time when Zeppelins (German airships) used to come above the field in front of our house. When they arrived, they lowered a basket down on a rope, and the basket would be full of delicacies, biscuits of every kind, chocolate and fruit. After the basket had come down low enough to be emptied, we filled it with butter, eggs and other things which they were pleased to have. The Zeppelins came every fortnight on a Thursday. No-one knew where they came from or where they returned to. Nothing good lasts for ever and that was true of these visits also. One day the Zeppelin circled around and started on the job of sending the basket down, but on the way back up, the rope caught on its side. The basket came free and fell on one of the dogs that were in the field and broke its leg. When the Zeppelin crew realised what had happened they sent a message saying that they would pay for the dog. The money came to the dog's owner, a sum much bigger than the value of the old dog. More than likely they had been frightened after seeing what had happened and also realised what the consequences would have been if it had fallen on one of the islanders. It was more than likely that the authorities knew nothing of the visits. Anyway we never saw them again.

VISITORS

Once, I remember, the ten children of Mr and Mrs Fenn, one of the lighthousekeepers, came to Bardsey for their holidays, and the name of every child finished with the same letter. Here is the list: Jaci, Judi, Harri, Mari, Emeli, Doli, Mali, Roni, Gweni and Lowri. There's a tribe for you and it wasn't an easy matter to find enough food to fill so many mouths. I wonder where some of these children have got to now. A pity we can't get together again after all these years and reminisce about the old days.

I'm sure I learned a lot of English in their company on the island. All of us on the island would have been much the poorer if the lighthousemen had not been there.

There was one young officer who came to Bardsey in connection with his work as lighthouse keeper and I took a fancy to this lad. As I grew a little older I used to look forward to seeing him on his return from Holyhead. The arrangement for the lighthousemen was two months on Bardsey then a month in Holyhead. When this boy was in Holyhead, he used to write a lot of letters to me. I received some of them, but I'm sure my father kept some.

When the boy returned to Bardsey one Saturday afternoon some kind of illness was troubling him and he decided to return with the boat to Holyhead. That was the last time I saw him. A message came to us not long after saying that he had passed away. Such are the ways of Providence, I suppose.

Some stories still stand out clearly in my memory, like the story of one of the lighthouse men. My sister and I found ourselves in a rather unpleasant situation. The man in charge of the lighthouse had arrived from Holyhead and by the look of him, I thought he was drunk. He was jumping over the gates and he made us run a race.

Shortly afterwards he came to one of the farms. The farmer's wife was busy making a pair of trousers for her boy. The man was deranged and totally set on putting on the trousers. Instantly the woman realised he was out of his mind.

He began to undress, like a madman again, and we had to look for men to help catch him and then tie him up so he couldn't move hand or foot.

After they'd got him under control, they tried to contact the boat by Morse Code and report the situation. They got hold of a doctor and a policeman and he was taken onto the boat and more than likely taken to an institution of some kind. A little while later we heard that he had died of some sickness like a brainstorm or some similar illness. He could easily have done us some injury.

Among the lighthouse people who came to Bardsey was Mr Baker who had married a French lady. One evening after they had come to the island I received an invitation to supper there and of course I was terribly pleased. I went there in good time, and after we'd talked for a little while it was announced that the meal was ready. We sat down at the table and it was covered with delicious things. I enjoyed them all, especially the soup. Then they invited us to go with them to see the garden. The wife was carrying a little basin in her hand and she started collecting snails in it, nasty big black snails. I tried to guess what she intended to do with them. I summoned up enough courage to ask her what she was going to do with the snails.

'Soup,' she said, 'like you had this evening. Did you enjoy it?'

As soon as I heard this explanation I turned on my heels and ran. On the way home I got rid of the soup and the rest of the supper. Thereafter when they called and invited me for supper there was nothing for it but to find an excuse and keep away from the lighthouse at mealtimes. For some weeks after that I couldn't bring myself to eat soup, even at home. I kept remembering the supper at the lighthouse.

DRIFTWOOD

Sometimes ships going past Bardsey would have cargoes of wood on deck and it was difficult to secure the wood so that it wouldn't be hurled into the sea by a storm. Sometimes the storm would come upon them and catch them unawares. Some of the load would be scattered and it would be impossible to retrieve the wood.

After the storm had scattered the ship's cargo, the elements would bring much of the wood to the shores of Bardsey. The word for this is driftwood.

This wood was suitable for repair work and useful for mending many things. We children greatly enjoyed collecting driftwood. We got up just before dawn and set off down to the rocks. Then we walked slowly along the slope and since the land was fairly flat along the shore it was easy to see into every cave. If there was a fairly big piece of wood it was hard work getting it from the clutches of the sea.

After a few days collecting driftwood and making heaps here and there on dry land, the owner of the wood would go along the shore to collect it all together. The wood was needed for several purposes, such as mending doors and many farm tools, and of course the boats as well. The small pieces would be used for kindling fires in the morning, as nothing was wasted.

Not far off Bardsey there's a stretch of sea called the 'Dead Sea'.

Yes, there's another place in the Middle East of the same name but Bardsey's Dead Sea is different. It's a place where at times the sea doesn't move except to turn on the spot. In this little whirlpool many logs can be seen spinning around without getting anywhere like a dog chasing its tail. When the fishermen had raised their pots, they would row to the Dead Sea on their way home and collect the wood which was swimming lazily there.

It wasn't only wood that washed up on Bardsey's shores. Some mornings walking along by the sea, we would have the sad experience of seeing a body washed up on shore and sometimes it would have been in the water a long time. If a body had been in seawater for weeks or months, it would look terrible. We were required to inform the authorities as they had to know about all bodies washed ashore. It didn't matter to what country it belonged. The islanders on Bardsey realised only too well that there was sadness in some home somewhere.

Part VI

THE EISTEDDFOD

Literary meetings used to be arranged on Bardsey fairly regularly. There was singing and reciting and lots of competitions. One man whom we thought could sing beautifully was John Griffith who moved here from Llanllawen Bach, Uwchmynydd. I used to sing in a quartet. The three who sang with me were Laura (Parc) Plas ym Mhenllech, Siôn Bron y Foel and Robin Dyno Goch.

The competitions were judged by the minister. The meetings, of course, were modelled on those held on the mainland. My father was by reputation a very good singer and he must have been, as he had been choir-master at Uwchmynydd chapel for a while before coming to Bardsey. He also trained our group and we often won.

Hardly a feast day went past without the inhabitants of Bardsey celebrating the occasion. They used to hold an Eisteddfod on St David's Day and to judge by the enthusiasm which was shown, Bardsey was second to none in celebrating the feast of the old Welsh Saint.

The minister always wanted everyone to compose one of the verses we call an englyn but unfortunately the poor chap knew nothing about the englyn, let alone teaching others to compose in *cynghanedd* (strict metre).

Here's a quotation from '*Y Genedl*':

'On the evening of Monday 3rd March nearly all the islanders came to the schoolhouse, to show their Welsh blood and to unite, in spirit at least, with the great family which was celebrating in the same way in every corner of the world. There is no danger of the old language dying on Bardsey. The danger on Enlli used to be that people thought there was no other language but Welsh. In spite of that, the children have been quick to learn English and their parents have now begun to realise that the world is bigger than Bardsey. It was a real Eisteddfod that was held on Bardsey, not just an evening of competitions. The Pwllheli committee will have to watch out, as the people of Bardsey have their eyes open and know full well what it means to hold an Eisteddfod in the grand manner. It is whispered that Bardsey is thinking of inviting the 1927 National Eisteddfod to the island. The king is all for it. Some people remember 'Mynyddog' coming to the island to adjudicate at an Eisteddfod and to sing, as only he could, of the dust of the bones of the old saints. Let us see what happens in 1927.'

Here's the programme of the Eisteddfod which was held on the evening of St David's Day. The islanders wanted the readers of '*Y Genedl*' to see it and also the names of the winners. (By the way, '*Y Genedl*' was the Bardsey paper, the only newspaper which came to the island.)

Recitation under 6. 'The little calf'	Jenny Pritchard
Recitation under 13. 'My faults'	Nellie Hughes
Open Recitation. 'The drunkard's daughter'	Nel Williams, Carreg
Singing under 6. 'Shepherd of Israel'	Sydna Hughes
Singing under 13. 'The little soldier'	Morfydd Evans
Singing under 15. 'Ned Puw's little granddaughter'	Griffith John Jones
Singing to the tune 'Cleveland'	Rachel Williams
Short story	Hugh Hughes
Three verses 'Ship in a storm'	Robert Williams, Carreg
Missing line competition	Nel Williams, Carreg
Essay 'Bardsey Today'	Evan Williams, Nant
Best wooden spoon	No prize awarded
Best basket	Robert Williams and Hugh Hughes equal first
Best picture of a draught horse	No prize awarded
Writing 'Nebuchadnezzar' on the blackboard with the left hand	Mary Williams and Maggie Hughes equal first
Two buttonholes — round and square	Mrs Hughes

Hemming a pocket handkerchief — Rachel Williams

In addition to the Eisteddfod and the competitions and the adjudications, a small choir sang, under the direction of Robert Williams, and the minister sang two songs. We also had an interesting debate between Rachel and Mary Williams. We had a lot of fun listening to them singing and acting. The competitions were judged by the minister and his wife and altogether they were kept very busy.

After about three hours of enthusiasm, jollification and entertainment, the Eisteddfod was brought to an end by us all singing the national anthem.

WORKING TOGETHER

On an island like Bardsey, with little more than 400 acres and only some ten families living there, there had to be unity. All of the inhabitants worked together, making their own laws and keeping to them to the letter. The most important law was that there should be no quarrels between one family and another, and I don't remember such a thing happening. Isn't it a pity that can't be the case today in the places where we've all settled down after leaving Bardsey!

One afternoon a message came to Bardsey that three men had arrived in Aberdaron, and planned to come to the island and collect the tithe monies. But the islanders weren't too happy when strangers like these came. Before starting out for Aberdaron, the islanders held a committee to discuss how to handle the three men.

This is the decision they came to. Whatever amount the tithe was to be, that would be the charge for fetching them and taking them back to Aberdaron. The total tithe was £36 and that was what the men had to pay before they started on their way back to Aberdaron.

MEDICAL MATTERS

If there was illness on the island, a doctor had to be fetched occasionally. But most frequently illnesses were cured by remedies made from herbs. I'm sure that Bardsey was a healthy place to live in.

My brother had pleurisy once and it was necessary to go across the Sound to fetch the doctor. On this occasion the wind got up, and there was no hope of them coming back to the island for about a fortnight. After the wind had dropped enough for the crew of the boat to come back to the island, who was there waiting for the boat but my brother.

My mother had been busy making bran poultices regularly and putting them on the affected part, and he recovered completely. There is no record of a doctor having lived on the island but I am sure that, had there been one, his pockets would have been fairly empty after his stay there.

If some relation from the Aberdaron area died, one of the inhabitants of Llŷn would light a fire on Mynydd Mawr, and then some members of the Bardsey families would cross by boat to ask who had passed away. If one of the inhabitants of Bardsey was poorly and needed a doctor, the crew of the boat would meet in the Anchorage and set off by boat to Aberdaron. After arriving there, one of the men would set off by bicycle to fetch the doctor and bring him back to Aberdaron, where the boat was waiting for him.

Then the boat was rowed back to Bardsey and the doctor could examine the patient. Then back to Aberdaron to bring the medicine back to Bardsey.

I have spoken of the wrath of the sea more than once and when someone was ill, it endangered the lives of the boat crew.

Some people suffered badly from seasickness, which made them feel really wretched. Once a teacher was coming back to Bardsey in the boat which had been over to get medicine for someone who was ill. The sea was exceptionally rough and they almost didn't make it. Waves were rising like huge walls around them, while the teacher lay in the bottom of the boat feeling really ill. Robat Bron y Foel asked her,

'Did you see how close the boat went to the rocks? We nearly came to an untimely end.'

'Indeed I didn't, and I'd prefer not to,' she replied.

I didn't have the doctor to see me on any occasion when I was living on Bardsey, although I had four operations after I left the island.

ILLNESS AND DEATH

My father was highly respected on the island because he could turn his hand to anything. He'd served his apprenticeship as a butcher and it was easy for him to kill cattle, pigs and sheep and cut them up very skilfully. Although he was skilled at killing animals, he was also just as skilled at alleviating a variety of illnesses with the help of old remedies.

I remember once we were obliged to get a vet for a mare we had, and the illness was colic. When the vet arrived on the island, it was easy to see that he'd had a drop too many before coming. After he'd finished seeing to the mare, my father said,

'We'll have to go now, Mr Tomos, the tide will not wait for anyone.'

'Well, go and tell it that its betters have had to wait for me in the past.'

My father was also a very good carpenter and used to make coffins and carts and a great many other things for the islanders. I remember once he was obliged to use the wood from a cart to make a coffin. I held a candle for him through the night. He made a very neat coffin and lined it with sailcloth and put a square piece of wood on the lid with a name carved on it.

THOMAS WILLIAMS
CARREG BACH
79 YEARS

Others had dug a grave and finished it with stones but the problem was how to lower the coffin down because there were no chains on it. After reflecting for a while inspiration came and he took the quilt from his bed, laid it on the ground and put the coffin on it. Then four men took hold of the corners of the quilt, carried it to the grave and lowered it neatly and respectfully. At the end someone offered to make a collection to pay my father for his work and the trouble he'd taken. I wonder if that's where the habit of making a collection during a funeral began?

I've already mentioned the Cristin family, Harri and Wil and Siân. Harri came home one day, lay down on the settle and died. On hearing of this, my father went over to offer his condolences on Harri's departure and Siân said in a really surly tone,

'Harri hasn't left us, he's lying on the settle, out of breath, that's all.'

My father wanted to measure him in order to make a coffin for him and she was saying there was no need because they would bury him in the garden in front of the house so they could still have his company.

'If you do that,' said my father, 'the police will be here.'

'Go home, lad, you and your policeman,' said Siân. Although my father thought he could handle people, he failed on this occasion and he had to go and fetch the minister. He succeeded in persuading her, and got Harri's tobacco pouch as a gift from Siân!

The Memorial Cross, Bardsey

Bardsey from Mynydd Mawr, inset of Love Pritchard.

Nel, Bessie and Wil

Landing cove, Bardsey

Bardsey, south end

Bardsey, bay and mountain

Carreg Fawr

Bardsey Chapel

Nel, Wil, Bessie and Ifor with Llew Hookes, Abersoch.

The Anchorage, Bardsey

Bardsey school children

Ifan in the back row of the boat (on far right) with some Bardsey residents.

Bardsey residents 1933

Bardsey's motor boat

Ifan, Nel, Bessie and Wil

The picture from John Pretoria.

Mr & Mrs Fen, who had 10 children.

Wil and Bessie (on the bike); Ifor (on the chair).

Four generations - both male and female

The lighthouse

Bardsey Chapel

Talcen y Foel

Nel, Ifan and Daniel at Gwenlli, Mynytho

Carreg Bach

Cristin

Porth Solfach

Part VII

BEREAVEMENT — MY WORLD TURNED UPSIDE DOWN

I have given some idea of my childhood on the island in the early years of this century. I went there when I was five, in the autumn of 1910, and I spent twelve years there until the end of 1922. That year our family suffered a terrible bereavement, when my mother was taken ill and went to Bangor hospital where she died.

For me, it was the end of the world. After the death I had to work very hard, looking after three men and my sister. Even now I don't know how I coped with all the work. There was milking and washing to be done, pigs to feed and bread to bake, but the hardest work was churning butter. All this work had to be done every day and it was easy to forget some job.

Many times during this period I was on my weary knees praying to God, desperately asking to be taken to mother. My words were answered. 'Ask and you shall receive' says the Bible. At first praying was nothing but a farce to me; no-one was listening to my prayers. As I grew older I realised that God was listening, and that He knew best and to this very day I believe in prayer although the answer might not come as I would wish.

In spite of everything I had to carry on with the work, and for quite a long period as well. Before long my brother Daniel left to go to sea, and my other brother Thomas went to Caernarfon to work. Then my sister Meri went to Fourcrosses (now called Y Ffôr). My father wasn't much help to me, as he used to go across to the mainland for long periods. We had to employ two lads to do the work on the farm. However, although there were these two farmhands, the responsibility always rested on my shoulders.

TUDWEILIOG — THE CYMANFA GANU
(*SINGING FESTIVAL*)

In spite of the difficult circumstances I grew up to be a young woman, dreaming of falling in love like every other girl. Once I was lucky enough to leave the island to go to the mainland and stay with an aunt who lived in Aberdaron. After I'd been there a few days there was a Cymanfa Ganu in Tudweiliog. It is still held there today. I was invited to the Cymanfa with my cousin and I looked forward eagerly to the event. I don't think I'd ever been to a Cymanfa Ganu before.

Every day seemed as long as a week, but in spite of that I knew it would soon come. At last the morning of the special day dawned and I was in high spirits. We got up and had breakfast and soon it was dinner-time. After we'd eaten we went and made ourselves look really smart and put on our Sunday best. The time came to walk down to the village to catch the bus which had been arranged to take us to the Cymanfa. I really enjoyed that journey, as I'd never been to Tudweiliog before.

As we got nearer to the chapel, we saw a huge crowd had gathered. Arriving there ourselves, we got off the bus and made our way towards the chapel. After we'd sat there for quite a while, two o'clock finally came. Men took their places in the deacons' pew and the pulpit and the meeting began, with everyone singing their heart out. Yes, I really enjoyed being in that meeting.

After a couple of hours the meeting came to an end and we left the chapel. During the service it had started raining very heavily, so the two of us made our way to the bus to shelter from the rain.

Maggie Nant, my companion that day, was a real character. There we were looking out of the bus window at the big crowd outside the chapel. As I looked out I saw one young lad and I turned to Maggie and said,

'Doesn't that boy standing out there look like Ifan John, Brynchwilog!'

What did madcap Maggie do but knock on the window to attract his attention and say,

'This girl here thinks you're very good-looking and she fancies you.'

I blushed right up to my ears and I didn't know where to look when he came up to us. After asking about this and that he said he'd come by bike with his friend Wil Pritchard. He said he worked on a farm in Deuglawdd, Aberdaron. He persuaded me to wait for him after the evening meeting.

When it was time for the second meeting to begin, there we were, the two of us, getting out of the bus and going back to the chapel. I didn't enjoy the singing much that evening, I couldn't stop thinking about the young lad and wondering if he would wait for me when we left the chapel.

The boy kept his promise and now it was my turn to ask questions of him. This was when he revealed his name, Ifan Williams originally from Rhoshirwaun. We didn't have a great deal of time to talk properly, because the bus was ready to leave and I was the last aboard.

I'd promised to write him a letter and I kept my promise. Following that we became closer friends and I used to go across from Bardsey as often as I could and he would come to Bardsey when he had the opportunity. I believe that meeting him was the happiest event in my life.

Each time the Annual Cymanfa is held at Tudweiliog, Bessie phones to say it's the Tudweiliog Cymanfa, and every time my answer is, 'If I'd stayed at home that day, think how much trouble I'd have been spared.' But the family know that I'm joking, to try and make Ifan jealous. It works too, because he's sure to snap back with something like, 'Why didn't you stick to one of your lighthouse keepers then: perhaps you'd have ten little lamps, and the lot of them howling like foghorns.'

When we managed to meet again, I learned that he'd been born in Hen Gorlan in the Rhoshirwaun district, one of the eight children of Roland and Janet Williams. I carried on seeing Ifan for quite a long period and the question of marriage often cropped up in the conversation.

Ifan had left school at the age of twelve. He got a job carrying flour on the Felin Fair mules. Incidentally at that time you had to pass an exam before being allowed to leave school. The work with the mules didn't last long as one Saturday evening, his employer asked him to go and boil food for the pigs, and this was Saturday night, would you believe! Ifan had been on the go since six o'clock in the morning. He simply packed his bag first thing Monday morning and went to work in the coalmines in South Wales. At the end of two years he came back to Llŷn to look for work as a farmhand. He got work at Mur Melyn farm, Rhoshirwaun and he was there until our marriage.

Part VIII

MOVING AGAIN

After a few months my father decided he wanted to leave Bardsey and come to live on the mainland. There was a bit of a problem bringing all the animals from Bardsey. No-one on the island was interested in the animals, but I think the main reason for this was that the inhabitants didn't want to see us turn our backs on the island.

We had an old dun mare and she would follow my father everywhere, so it was very easy to get her onto the boat. After my father had walked onto the boat she followed him without any fuss.

It was really slow work carrying everything down to the Anchorage, ready to load it onto the boat. We had to carry all the furniture and also drive each group of animals in turn. We were moving from Carreg, which was a really big house to live in a much smaller cottage, so my father held an auction in Aberdaron village to sell some of the furniture.

We didn't get much for the old mare. She was afraid of everyone but my father, and she didn't live very long after moving. Perhaps she felt homesick for Bardsey, as we did, or perhaps she was too nervous. If the mare longed to be back on Bardsey, so did I. I didn't miss the hard work but a wave of nostalgia would come over me when I remembered the pleasant and amusing times we had on the island.

My father became friendly with another woman from Aberdaron. He'd decided we would leave the island and he bought his old home, Grepach, Uwchmynydd. He paid about £400 for it, I think and there were a few acres of land with the house too. When people left the island they would leave many things for the new tenants.

Some people have suggested that the islanders used to marry each other, but in twenty-six years I saw no-one getting married there except for my brother who married one of the local girls who lived on the island.

After about two years my father married and I felt uneasy, seeing another woman taking my mother's place in the home. But of course as I was courting seriously and was head over heels in love, I was now very much happier. I only thought about one thing, namely marrying the comely young lad and starting a new period in my life.

MARRYING IFAN

Very soon a day was appointed for Ifan and I to be married. I'd thought so much about that ceremony, and looked forward to the all important day. We were married in Eglwys Newydd, Aberdaron in 1925. After the wedding we were invited to my father's home in Grepach for the wedding breakfast and all credit to my step-mother, she prepared a wonderful meal.

After about a year, in August 1925, William John our first son was born. By then we had set up home in Tŷ Hen (later called Tegfan). Tŷ Hen is very close to Talcen-y-Foel. Whether I felt some longing to go back to Uwchmynydd, or whether it was all pure chance, I don't know.

After getting married, I hadn't a penny to my name and hardly a shirt on my back. I went to stay with Ifan's sister for a little while. Then on to Tŷ Hen, Uwchmynydd. While I was there I had no money, and lived on boiled potatoes.

There was a character living in Uwchmynydd when we were in Tŷ Hen who had a pony, and the old rascal was too miserly to give her any food. The pony was sick one day and he just had to call the vet. Up to the house comes Tomos the vet.

'Where's your pony?'

He took Tomos to the hut where the pony was, and of course the vet saw at once what was the matter. So he asked, 'Have you got any whisky?'

'No' was the reply.

'Well, go and get some from Aberdaron.'

He set off hurriedly in that direction. The vet went to the house to have a cup of tea, and told them to boil the kettle. Before long, the whisky arrived from Aberdaron. Yes, you're right. The vet drank all the whisky, and gave the hot water to the pony, saying he needed the whisky more than the pony did.

I didn't hate living in Tŷ Hen; after all it was our home at a time when there wasn't much choice of empty houses in the locality. It was somewhere for us to live for a while. By this time Ifan had left Methlem Farm and had gone to Cors y Wlad, Sardis, where he earned an extra shilling a week on his wages.

This was the hardest time I had in my whole life, I'm sure. We were very poor, as people of our age will know. But we weren't the only poor ones as most people were poor in the locality at that time.

Sometimes Ifan would stay in Cors y Wlad, Sardis, throughout the week and come home to me on Saturday afternoons, going back after dinner on Sunday. The journey was quite a distance, about twenty miles each way, and that's how far he had to travel each week on his bike, all because his wages were a shilling a week higher there than in Llŷn.

Often he came home soaked to the skin after pedalling on his bike against the elements. It was difficult not to get soaked on a bike, in the wind and the rain. But it's not like that today, when you can get plenty of suitable clothing for going out in a storm. In the end, this travelling caused some strain between the two of us and after a little persuasion Ifan agreed to come and live in the paradise of Bardsey.

From that moment on I longed for the day when I would be able to return to that idyllic place. If I was feeling downcast, the very thought of it would bring joy to my heart. To make things even better, word came that our old home was empty. That's luck for you, to be able to set up home again in Carreg Fawr. I couldn't have wished for anything better. Yes, to make a fresh start where there had been so much sadness at one time. A chance to start again, this time in joy and gladness.

BACK TO BARDSEY

Moving our belongings wasn't much of a job the first time, as we didn't own very much.

When we'd been on Bardsey for a while, we spent a few years on the mainland again before returning to the island a second time. The inhabitants had changed a lot, with families leaving and other families taking their place and now I can give a list of those who were living there:

Carreg Bach — John Thomas, carpenter and his family.

Tŷ Pella — Tomos Griffith and his family.

Dyno Goch — Huw and Doris Williams and their children, and later William and Mary Jones and their children.

Cristin — John and Jane Evans and family.

Plas Bach — a family who moved to Plas ym Mhenllech, near Tudweiliog in Llŷn, and later Jack and Lisi Jones. Also the minister, Rev. Edward Evans, was a lodger.

Tŷ Nesaf — Sam Jones and his wife and children.

Tŷ Bach — Griffith and Lizzie Jones and their two daughters.

Tŷ Capel — Mrs Murray Williams, the teacher and her family.

Tŷ Pella — William and Nellie Evans and their daughter.

And us, Nel and Ifan Williams, in Carreg Fawr.

During this period a plan was launched for people to contribute the sum of three shillings and threepence a quarter, which gave families the right to treatment in the hospital in Bangor without any additional payments.

We also contributed towards the wages of the local nurse. When these arrangements were suggested nearly every family took advantage of the service.

Part IX

OCCUPATIONS — WORK FOR IFAN

The two main occupations on Bardsey were farming and fishing. The quality of the land was exceptionally good with everyone using seaweed as manure. While we were there we saw only one sackful of artificial fertiliser being used. Today more and more people are using organic fertiliser on their land. Indeed the farmers from Llŷn would wait in Pwllheli market for Bardsey barley to arrive in order to use it as seed-corn. Some of the land was also kept for growing gorse, the finely mashed young shoots being valuable for the animals, while the stumps were used as fuel — nothing was wasted. There were also osiers growing there, these being used to make lobster-pots and baskets, with almost everybody skilled at this task.

Cattle were kept for milk and calves were raised and taken to Aberdaron to sell. There were also sheep, for raising lambs and producing wool to make clothes. I don't remember whether anyone used to spin or not. Of course, fattening pigs also brought an occasional penny into the coffers.

Then there was fishing. Fish were caught off the rocks or by boat so we could have a fresh fish for supper. Also pots were put out to catch lobsters and crabs. These of course were sent to places on the mainland and we could rely on them making a profit throughout the summer. It wasn't worth trying to catch lobsters during the winter because the weather smashed the pots and made us lose money.

There was no enmity amongst the fishermen on Bardsey. They

all helped each other. Once some French boats came and anchored in the Rhonllwyn, a small bay near the Anchorage. The crew seemed a friendly lot, they kept bringing scent and bottles of wine for us and we thought they were nice people.

Yes indeed, really nice people. Then everyone realised that they were trespassing, putting out their lobster pots close to the shore instead of keeping three miles off shore, as required by the authorities.

And what happened on the next visit of the ship which had broken the fishing laws? The fishermen all went out in their boats, lifted all the pots and brought them back to their farms. That was the last we saw of the French fishermen round the coast of Bardsey.

There was a good price, even during that period, to be had from lobsters. Here are the yields for two years, 1926 and 1930. In 1926 5520 crabs were caught and fetched £74. Then four years later 3324 crabs were caught, with a value of £42. In 1926 4968 lobsters worth £207 and in 1930 2796 lobsters worth £116.

There's some inconsistency in the figures, but perhaps in some years the weather was rougher and that made it more difficult to go out and lift the catch on board. In spite of that the earnings were quite good at that time.

One day an opportunity came for Ifan to go and work for the lighthouse people. This happened in 1927 and he accepted the offer.

WORK FOR IFAN

Ifan was lucky to get work in the lighthouse, doing repairs like painting, fixing doors and other small jobs there. One job he had was to put a new roof on the foghorn room. This work was done in an exposed spot where there wasn't much shelter from the wind. He also had to work after it had got dark. Of course there wasn't any electricity there and he had to work for some hours by the light of a hurricane lamp, the only sort of light that could withstand the weather. The man who was in charge of the workers was very dark-skinned and everyone called him Boss. He was easy to get along with. High on his list was a fondness for whisky. One day he asked Ifan to go to the galley and get him a bottle, so he went and when he got there he found the cook and the galley boy had drunk the lot and were rolling drunk.

When the Boss was told, he blew his top and went and got a gun with two cartridges in it, saying he intended to shoot one of them that night. It was lucky for him that the lads in the lighthouse saw him and they charged off after him and took the gun off him.

I can't quite remember the names of all the lighthouse keepers. But one does come to mind readily, a Mr Bachelor, from around 1912. We thought highly of him because he was the man who made a brass fender for my mother and father. To this day I regret that I left it behind when I moved away from the island.

Although a lot of different people looked after the lighthouse, some came fairly regularly and some just for a short stay. Here are the names of some who came to the island: Payne, Watts, Fen and Sunaway.

Visitors to the island were unable to understand how we were able to put up with the deafening sound of the foghorn, but they also got used to the sound very quickly.

At the start of the century, and for some years afterwards, the lighthouse got oil from a ship and there were at least two ships doing the work, the Beacon and the Patricia. After they'd dropped anchor they loaded the boat with large barrels of oil and brought them ashore and then the cart was filled with the barrels and it carried them up to the lighthouse.

One day, when the sun was hot, the ship had brought a load of oil ashore. The cart was loaded and had started off along the road, when halfway through the journey the horse started jibbing and nothing would make him go backwards or forwards. Seeing the horse had stopped, the lighthouse keeper came to see what was the matter. Seeing the pickle Ifan was in, he said that he had something in the house that would solve the problem. Before long he came back with a small box and told Ifan to put some of the powder from it, namely pepper, under the horse's tail. Ifan did as the man said but the horse didn't move. In the end they had to haul the load to the lighthouse with a rope.

One day in the lighthouse they had the job of using block and tackle to lower some big tanks down but the rope got stuck in the block. The boss had seen what was the matter and told them how to free the rope. After the boss had gone, they hauled on the rope, but instead of it coming free, the tanks crashed down with a deafening noise that echoed all over the island. The lighthouse lads were watching what was happening and shouting 'Keep clear' as it was dangerous to be close to tanks of this weight.

Love Pritchard worked in the lighthouse with Ifan, and on that day he needed a loaf from Carreg. While he was walking down to the house from the road he started crying and I saw him and thought surely something must have happened in the lighthouse, as I'd heard the noise. I was convinced that Ifan was badly hurt or was dead. But luckily he was only playing a trick on me.

Another of Ifan's jobs in the lighthouse was to go into the big tank to paint it. It was Thanksgiving week and the Welshman who was working with Ifan had gone to the service. The boss asked Ifan if he wanted to go to the Thanksgiving and Ifan got time off to go there. There was another Welshman working with Ifan, called Twm Bach Llanbedrog (near Pwllheli). I can't remember his full name. Each summer a man called Ifan Wright, who owned a big sailing boat, used to call on the island. One day when the yacht had come to Bardsey, Twm asked the boss if he could go home for a week. No-one could stop him going home, but getting his cards was the price Twm paid for going against the boss' wishes.

FURNITURE

When we went to live on Bardsey, we didn't have much furniture, especially bedroom furniture. I knew there was a shop in Pwllheli that sold second hand furniture. After crossing to the mainland, Ifan went all the way to Pwllheli and arriving there, walked to John Pretoria's shop. (I don't know his full name.) Ifan went in to see

John who was at that time about to retire. John asked Ifan where he lived and so on, chatting and enquiring for some time and then he came out with 'Since you're a regular chapel-goer, you can have what bedroom furniture I've got for nothing.' He gave him a family Bible as well, together with a pretty picture of two roses with a verse from the Bible. I've recently given the picture to Bessie, my daughter, who will be mentioned later on.

On the island there were a lot of horses working on the farms, with some farms keeping two horses. Eight horses were ferried from Aberdaron to Bardsey in the big boat in a fairly short period. Of the eight, one horse was lost when it jumped over the side of the boat into the sea. The owner had flatly refused to tie the horse's feet, which was the custom. Possibly, if the boatmen had rowed more carefully and slowly, it would have arrived safely. But in any case the sea was very rough, they said.

COMING AND GOING TO THE MAINLAND

Usually it was the men who went across to the mainland to fetch goods and food. Sometimes some of the women would want underwear. Their husbands were too embarrassed or too shy to fetch such items from William Ifan's shop in Aberdaron, so Ifan would undertake this job himself.

When Ifan was a farmhand on a farm called Mur Melyn in Rhoshirwaun, the farmer there, Robin Mur Melyn, used to say, 'Let's go over to Bardsey', so they dropped what they were doing and set off for Bardsey.

Robin was the owner of a fairly large boat and used to carry day trippers to Bardsey.

Only very occasionally would we go up onto Bardsey Mountain apart from on sheep-rounding days or going with ferrets to catch rabbits. No-one was happy about the children going to the top of the mountain as it was a very dangerous place for the inexperienced.

Part X

AGRICULTURE AND COMMUNICATION

According to tradition there are twenty thousand saints buried on Bardsey, and one can well believe it. When ploughing and tilling the fields, there were bones scattered everywhere, just like the cemetery. Ifan had a shock one day when he was out with his mare, ploughing the land. All of a sudden the mare slipped into a grave, and there was the skull of a young girl with curly blond hair still on it.

The folk on Bardsey weren't bothered about transport, they were well accustomed to walking miles along the length and breadth of the island. Of course if you had to carry something which was really heavy, there was always a horse at hand to put between the shafts of the cart.

I saw one bike on the island and that belonged to my son William. It was a tricycle given to him as a Christmas present. The children all spent long hours having fun with the bike. The only snag was there were gates separating one farm from the next. It was a bit of a nuisance having to open and shut the gates. Jane Ifans, Cristin saw William on his tricycle and he very nearly knocked her over. She told William off and muttered, 'He'll be the death of us all with that bike of his!'

During those years things on Bardsey were improving in many respects. We learned one thing of great value — how to communicate with the mainland, through two of the islanders learning how to speak with a lamp. Yes, this was a real blessing when we wanted a doctor to come across to Bardsey.

This means of communication was used for many years. Of course if there was mist or drizzle it was impossible to see the light. It was particularly valuable when my daughter was in hospital. Ifan could get information regularly about her condition. One thing that bothered the speakers was the cold, and so in the end it was decided to build two little sheds with windows and a place for the lamp, one at Pen Cristin on Bardsey and the other near Pen Bryn Bach, Uwchmynydd. Although these sheds were rather rough, still they managed to keep the cold out.

When we had more or less mastered this skill, we had great fun from time to time establishing contact with ships which happened to be passing Bardsey and asking them about their voyage. Once we got a response from a ship on its way to Liverpool.

'Who's speaking?' I said.

'Robin Tŷ Nant, Aberdaron' came the reply.

Amazing that I'd chosen that ship, wasn't it? Robin was my cousin.

FAMOUS VISITORS

In our second period on Bardsey we had very many visitors who came to enjoy a few days or sometimes weeks of leisure.

For instance Rev. Tom Nefyn Williams, George M. Ll. Davies and his brother Stanley and the family, and Professor Glyn Davies, author of 'Cerddi Portinllaen'. I'm sure that everyone knows the song:

> 'Gwen and Mair and Elin
> Are eating lots of pudding
> And little Benji's going daft
> And howling most uncommon.'

Gwen and Mair and Elin were three sisters and Benji was the name of their dog. All of them stayed with us on Bardsey and we have kept in close touch with each other to this day. Gwen and Mair are in America and Elin in South Wales.

When the weather permitted, ships would come laden with

trippers, fairly large ships, with thick ropes hung around the ship to prevent damage when it docked. These ships were called paddle-steamers because they were driven by a wheel behind the ship similar to a water wheel. These ships would anchor off Bardsey, as many as three of them in a day. The visitors were unable to come ashore and so it was the task of the islanders to carry them in their own little boats back and forth from the ship.

The boat owners didn't charge any fee but accepted whatever was given them and made a fair pocketful by the end of the day. Sometimes about four hundred day-trippers would come. Once on the island, they would look for somewhere to get a cup of tea and a bite to eat. By the end of the day everybody's food cupboard would be almost empty and we had to go to Aberdaron to stock up on more victuals.

THE THRESHER

The young men knew there was a real need for a threshing machine on the island. This monster was used in many places in the countryside to separate the grain from the chaff. They started discussing the matter and before long the fruits of the discussion were seen. Some of the young men crossed to the mainland with the intention of buying a thresher. They'd heard of one for sale near Dolgellau. After discussing the price they agreed to pay about sixty pounds. They arranged to get a lorry to bring the thresher to Aberdaron. After it was unloaded it stayed there until there was a favourable day for bringing it to the island.

Before long the day came. The young men got up very early, went across in the largest boat they had and arrived in Aberdaron before dawn. The seven of them were ready to give it a go, come what may.

Before they could start loading they had to find some strong timbers and place them across the boat to keep the thresher secure. They had to be extremely careful, slow and cautious, so as not to damage the boat or its load. When dawn broke, the day was fine and the sea like glass, not a wave anywhere, ideal weather for crossing the Sound with the valuable load. You have probably heard of the Loch Ness monster; I wonder if some of the early risers of Aberdaron and round about thought they had seen something of the same kind.

The Anchorage was reached safely, and the older inhabitants were amazed that the venture had succeeded. It meant no-one would need to thresh by hand any more.

PROVISIONS

Here I would like to talk about how we got provisions. Two bags of flour were bought for every family every fortnight, or rather eggs and butter were bartered in Aberdaron for the flour. Everyone on the island had their own butter stamp. It said, 'Carreg Farm Bardsey' on our stamp. Sometimes we bought yeast but often we made yeast ourselves. There were plenty of hops on the island, they only needed gathering at the right time; I can hardly remember food ever being scarce there.

There were plenty of fish, crabs, lobsters, chickens, geese, ducks, beef cattle, sheep and pigs. Every farm would kill animals in turn and share the meat. Each farm would make an excellent feast for the islanders, everyone vying to do better than everyone else. In that meal there would be plenty of beef, pork or lamb, roast potatoes, vegetables and rice pudding made slowly in the oven by the fire and plum pudding in a bag (like Christmas pudding boiled in a white cloth).

We would have a real feast that day, some overeating and slipping into heavy sleep, others being affected in quite a different way, unable to shut their eyes but labouring through the night with stomach pains and unable to eat anything for days — a real 'Pigs' Supper'.

Part XI

FISHING

We had to have fish-meat as bait in the pots to attract the lobsters. It was easy to fish from the rocks and catch wrasse, a bait which is very attractive to lobsters, but Ifan, poor soul, fought shy of going because he felt the rocks were moving under him. He wasn't too fond of walking across the rocks to look for crabs in the crevices either.

Generally the fishermen threw out a net to catch wrasse as bait for the pots. Ifan and John Cristin would throw out a net near the shore at Traeth Ffynnon and get a netful of wrasse in a very short time.

It was really hard work setting the pots to catch lobsters and crabs. The pots were heavy to lift as there were three stones (three fairly big rocks) tied to each pot. The men had to lift some pots with nothing in them, and move them to a different place, hoping for better luck tomorrow. They spent hours in the boat rowing from pot to pot with hardly a break. When they'd finished checking the pots they had to put all the lobsters in a closed pot so that they couldn't escape. They had to do the same with the crabs. The lobsters brought in more money than the crabs, although the price at that time was low compared with today. We used to get tenpence for each lobster and fourpence for each crab.

Of course I'm talking about money at the start of the century. We had to pay sixpence for getting each boxful to Pwllheli, though we very often had complaints that the lobsters had died and were no use. But the ones we sent to Manchester, they were alive and well when they arrived. Can you explain that?

Sometimes one of the islanders would see something unusual happening, and on such an occasion everyone else would have to go and see for themselves. One day Ifan and his friend went out fishing in a boat. They saw a small boat going past and none of the crew to be seen anywhere. Ifan wanted to go on board the boat but his friend was adamant he wouldn't go.

A few days later we found out about the boat. Some men from the mainland had gone on board and sailed her to Abersoch, and they got a good reward from the owner when he got his boat back undamaged.

Part XII

BIRTH AND ILLNESS

On the 4th of April, 1930 our daughter Bessie was born. I went over to the mainland about a fortnight before she was born to stay with Ifan's sister, whose house was a little way from Sarn Mellteyrn, at Pig Parc. After her birth I was at the farm for another fortnight before bringing my little girl back to Bardsey. On returning to the island I had to carry on with my work as before. William was now at school on Bardsey.

One Borth Fair day when Bessie was four, she was taken very ill. This was a very distressing time for us as a young family, the most miserable time we had on the island. Every parent knows what it's like to watch a child suffer.

As normally happened when there was illness and a doctor was needed, the boat set off quickly across the Sound to get the doctor. The journey wasn't over when we reached Aberdaron, we had to go on to Botwnnog to see if the doctor was there. Luckily he was and he came to Aberdaron as quickly as he could.

Having landed the boat on Bardsey we had to lead the young doctor, who was suffering from dreadful seasickness, up to the little girl at Carreg. In a few minutes the doctor said,

'Bangor Hospital, straightaway, there isn't a minute to lose, her appendix is about to burst.'

We wrapped Bessie in a blanket that instant and carried her down to the Anchorage to the boat where the crew were ready to row back to Aberdaron. It was touch and go because the sea turned rough, and Ifan and Wil couldn't return for a fortnight.

We got to Aberdaron, hired John Pensarn's taxi to take us on to Bangor and my aunt, Meri Gwenallt, came in her apron and held Bessie on her knee throughout the journey to Bangor. The village of Aberdaron was full of people who'd heard about the sick girl and had seen the Bardsey boat bringing over the emergency case.

The doctor phoned Bangor to make sure there was a doctor there to receive the patient and that the theatre was ready for Bessie's operation.

When we reached the hospital, my little girl was taken away from me to have the operation as quickly as possible. Aunt Meri went home in the taxi, but I stayed in Bangor for six weeks. I was really fortunate as I was invited to stay with the Davies family who used to come to us for their summer holidays on the island. I am greatly indebted to them for all their kindness.

This was the most worrying time that Ifan ever had. He had to return to Bardsey without any of us as I was in Bangor with Bessie and William was with relatives in Aberdaron. Although Ifan couldn't cross to Bardsey for a fortnight, he didn't need to worry, as he knew the islanders would look after everything. As nobody on the island ever locked a door, the islanders could do all that was necessary.

At that time Ifan was the chapel treasurer, and he kept the money in a bowl on the top of the dresser. Although there was quite a sum of money there, not one penny went missing. What would happen today, I wonder? I'm sure there isn't a more honest place anywhere. It's easy to understand why life on Bardsey was so happy when we could live surrounded by such honesty. If there are twenty thousand saints buried there, there were a fair number of saints living there as well.

When someone had been caught on the mainland and couldn't get back to Bardsey because the weather was unfavourable, the custom was to share. Yes, people shared out everything which wouldn't keep, like butter, milk and eggs. If no churning was done, the milk would soon go to waste. When the weather was good enough for the family to come back, there would be a roaring fire waiting for them in the hearth, the house would be beautifully warm and the inhabitants would bring plenty of food for them.

When the three of us came back to the island, you never saw a welcome like the one we had, everyone cuddling Bessie and giving her all sorts of presents. Yes indeed, she was really spoiled. On that occasion Bessie received more presents than she ever had in her life, about fourteen dolls, and one big dolly from Mrs McCowen and her family of Carreg Plas, Aberdaron. It was an especially pretty doll dressed as a bride. We tried to hang the doll on the wall so that everyone could see it, but we didn't manage to.

MISCHIEF

One Sunday morning when Ifan and Bessie had gone to chapel and we were at home with William, busy preparing dinner, one of the lighthouse keepers called in, as they did occasionally while out for a walk. As soon as he was in the house he said he could smell burning from somewhere and went through to the parlour. What did we see but the dolly burning and William running away as fast as his legs could carry him. A little later he confessed that he was responsible for the doll going up in flames in the parlour.

'That girl gets everything and I get nothing,' he said.

It was easy to understand his jealousy because she'd received too much attention when she was ill. After her stay in hospital, Bessie always wanted to play doctors and nurses.

One day the two had searched for all the dolls, and had gone off with them to play doctors and nurses, giving each one an appendix operation. When they realised what they had done to the dolls, there were tears on their cheeks for a long time.

I remember another time we had to get a doctor to her. She had come across some glass balls under the dresser which had floated onto the shore, green glass balls that were so smooth that you could see your reflection in them. Bessie grabbed one and ran out with it, but unfortunately she tripped and the ball was smashed to pieces and we had to take her to have stitches in her mouth. Bessie was a bit of a chatterbox at that time, but after this scrape she had to be quiet for a very long time.

You had to be careful what you said when she was around. There was a Welshman who came to the lighthouse and he would always be making a song and dance, going on and on about how poor he was. We would very often give a nickname to someone if something had happened and he too got a nickname, namely The Church Mouse. One day when he walked over to our house, as soon as Bessie saw him, she shouted out at the top of her voice, 'Mam, the Church Mouse has arrived.'

Another day the minister, Rev. Edward Evans (the last to serve on the island), went to fetch two buckets of water for me, and every time he stooped to lift the water, Bessie threw fine gravel at his bald pate. Evans was hopping mad and when he got hold of her, he almost strangled her, and if it hadn't been for me coming into sight, I honestly believe he would have killed her. It was as if he had lost all control of himself. He shook his head and said very gruffly, 'You've brought up a wonderful boy, but as for this girl, I don't know what will become of her.'

A little baby had been born in Tŷ Bach who wasn't healthy at all. He was plagued with convulsions and the doctor was called to see him. The doctor came but regrettably he said that there was no hope for him. That baby died.

I only remember four others who died and were buried on the island.

HOME SICKNESS

Many people have thought that living on Bardsey is like being in heaven, but that isn't always the case. A young minister once came to the island to look after his flock, but soon he was homesick for the mainland. While sitting in the calm tranquility of the mountainside, he set down his experience in verse, and this is the longing that was in his heart:

> 'On the quiet mountainside
> Far away from city noise
> Stood a very shy young lad
> Listening hard for human voice.
> Hiraeth rose within his heart
> And his sighs covered the land.
> With his longing came the wish
> That his release be close at hand.'

I'm not sure whether he was called to minister elsewhere but more than likely he went somewhere on the mainland.

Once when William was very little, the two of us were in the bedroom. Ifan had gone to chapel and from the bedroom we heard a great snorting sound. We couldn't work out what was happening. Going out of the bedroom what did we see at the bottom of the stairs but a bull that had gone mad. I was terrified and thought I would die of fright. What should I do? I had no idea.

Our luck changed when the dog turned up from somewhere and started barking. At that the bull turned and rushed out as fast as it could, and chased after the dog. As for us, we watched the race from the bedroom window, the dog leading the way, his feet working harder than they'd ever worked before. The bull then tried to catch him, without success. We were still much too frightened to go downstairs and stayed in the bedroom until Ifan came back.

The bull was the Plas Bach bull, the only one on the island. Its services were used by all the farms because there was no such thing as A.I. in those days. As it had gone mad, the butcher from Aberdaron had to come to slaughter it.

When he came over, we had quite a job getting the bull into the shed but after a long time it went in. Then the butcher climbed in through the window of the corn loft and made his way slowly across the cross beam (a strong piece of wood holding up the roof). When he reached a point above the bull, he waited quietly for a chance to drop down onto the bull's back and push the knife point into its throat. What would the matadors of Spain think of such a thing, I wonder? The butcher's opinion was that the bull had got sunstroke and that it had the effect of making him go mad.

I was often asked if I was afraid of drowning. Goodness gracious, no. It's much safer travelling across the Sound than to Pwllheli by car. Perhaps there are more fools with vehicles than with boats.

Ifan had been in Aberdaron getting something to sharpen a razor which had become very blunt and couldn't cut the beard cleanly. He came back and forgot to change his coat before going to sea with William Hugh. When he was in the boat, he realised the razor was in his pocket. He pulled the razor out and opened it and showed it to William Hugh and then asked him, 'Is there anything you want to do before I finish you off with my razor?' William was extremely frightened, thinking Ifan was in earnest.

When we were on Bardsey a boat named Ynys Enlli (*Bardsey Island*) was brought over, to be used by the inhabitants. Before long, when it had been on the water for a certain time, it needed to be checked over and as instructed, the men took it to Pwllheli.

After some days we had word that the boat was ready and the men went to fetch it. At the start of the journey back to Bardsey, the boat and the engine were working well. After reaching Cilan Head near Abersoch, the weather turned nasty and as the wind was in the east, nobody knew what would become of the boat in the dangerous waves. As one man, the crew decided to turn back and make for the shore at Abersoch.

The next morning the wind and the sea had quietened. After getting the boat into the water, they tried to start the engine, but not a chance. They got an engineer there and he saw that there was not one drop of oil in the engine. Someone had forgotten to put clean oil in it. In the end they succeeded in starting the engine and they came home safely. If the engine had stopped working at Cilan, the crew would have drowned.

As circumstances had improved by then, and the islanders had a new boat with an engine in it to fetch what they needed for Aberdaron, there was no need to use the wooden rowing boat which was exhausting to row. The boat served all the islanders and one of the inhabitants was responsible for it and Ifan made sure there was enough petrol all the time.

Although things were improving on the island, another problem raised its head. We heard that the school was going to close. What would happen to the children?

In 1930 when my cousin gave birth to a son the woman who attended to her was remarkably scatty. The first thing she did when the little boy was born, was place him in my arms before he'd been fed. I had such a fright I fell to the floor in a faint and I was still in a faint when the doctor came to the house. He blew his top with the nurse and said some very nasty things to her and gave her a scolding. Her action could have been enough to make me lose Bessie. But by some miracle nothing happened.

No-one learned new crafts on the island but the boys learned how to handle boats and how to read the weather signs. The children in the school learned all sorts of things and I remember a man once came to teach us children how to knit with one needle and he had a needle with him specially made for knitting ties.

Many of the children managed to knit something under his instruction. He was an ugly old man to our eyes, with smallpox scars. His clothes weren't smart either and he asked us children for kisses and this frightened us. When all's said and done he wasn't as bad as all that, and he brought lots of oranges and apples for us.

There's an old tradition that it brought bad luck if a corpse or coffin was taken away by ship or boat, but for the people of Bardsey no such thing as superstition existed.

A lot of people have asked about Christmas on the island. At that time of year life revolved around the lighthouse, where the children used to get presents from the lighthouse men. We had to remember that Santa would be calling. Parents would make sure that there were things to fill the stockings the week before Christmas.

The family from Carreg Plas, Aberdaron would make sure that enough fruit and sweets came to the island each year. As everywhere else, everyone bustled about preparing for the festivities.

One Christmas Day one of our cattle went to Ffynnon Baglau (*Spring of the Crutches*) and above the spring there is a high rock. The cow slipped off the rock and broke her leg, or at any rate injured it badly. It was said that the water from this spring was very beneficial for complaints of the feet and legs. Also it was to this spring that pilgrims used to go to cure any kind of affliction in their legs. After being cured, they would throw away their crutches on Bryn Baglau (*Crutches Hill*).

After persevering for hours and as always with the help of neighbours, the cow was pulled out of the spring. She was fine when she went there, but she certainly needed crutches after they'd succeeded in getting her out. The poor thing was very lame indeed.

One Christmas we heard on the only radio set on the island that the inhabitants of Bardsey were starving. The report said that there was no food on the island and that people across the whole of Wales were praying for them. The newspapers were full of the story. However the situation was not as bad as that. People had forgotten that Bardsey was nearly self-sufficient. There was enough meat, butter, milk, eggs and vegetables of every kind and everyone shared when necessary.

Looking back across the years, I can't remember ever getting mackerel like the ones that were to be had in the sea around the island. Today they don't have the same taste at all. If the weather was quite hot they used to catch mackerel, then clean them and put them on the zinc roof of one of the sheds to bake in the sun. Their flavour still lives in my memory, that glorious flavour that was much better than the fried ones you get nowadays. Moreover, as is emphasised today, it was food cooked without using any fat.

With the mackerel baked in the sun on top of the shed with the zinc roof, one problem which arose was that you had to be on the lookout all the time they were there. Every seagull on the rocks of Bardsey realised there was a good dinner to be had in Carreg without any of them having to get their feet wet.

At Christmas time there was a goose for dinner with all the kinds of vegetables available on the island. Then Christmas pudding with sweet butter. The only things the children had in their stockings were oranges and apples as there was not a lot of money about.

The children of Y Nant used to receive a lot of presents on Christmas Day. There was plenty of money at Y Nant, since their family worked on the mainland and received good wages.

One day most of the men, including Ifan, went on their regular trip to the mainland. When they'd done their shopping in Aberdaron, they set off back to the island. On the way back they saw another boat coming to meet them. They turned the nose of the boat to meet the other boat. William our son had had an accident. He was busy with some machine or other and his finger got stuck in some cogs on the machine when William Cristin was turning the handle. He'd hurt his finger a little bit.

A bit of a baby, that was always our opinion of William. There was something the matter with him, but he wasn't really ill. The doctor said that sea air was definitely not good for him. It was proved that sea breezes didn't suit him when we left the island for the second time. Yes, the doctor was quite right because once we'd left Bardsey, William was perfectly well.

In January 1935 another son was born to us, and as before, I was able to go and stay with an aunt for a fortnight before the birth. Then I stayed for another two weeks before returning to Bardsey. The day I was going home from the mainland, I was standing on the beach waiting for the boat. Before the boat landed, some old fellow asked me, 'What's the little boy's name?'

'Well,' I answered, 'we've not chosen a name yet.'

'Well,' he said looking at the sea which was quite rough, 'he's going *i fôr gwyn* (into a white sea).'

'Ifor Wyn. Yes, Ifor Wyn,' I said to myself. 'Yes, that'll be his name.'

I've talked about Porth Solfach, the harbour which is opposite the Anchorage, but it's not an ideal place to keep boats in. Sometimes the wind would get up fairly quickly, especially from the east and it would be very difficult to control the boats against the wind. When this happened the boats would make for shelter in Porth Solfach, although it was a terribly dangerous place for those unfamiliar with it, as I have already said, as there were sharp rocks there, which could damage wooden boats.

Hardly anyone went to bed very late. We had to get plenty of sleep at night as the men had to get up fairly early sometimes, to get out to sea when the tides were right. I used to go and fetch William Huw every morning to go out to sea with Ifan. Perhaps he suffered from lie-in-itis.

Accidents can sometimes happen, like the one that occurred on the Sound side of Bardsey Mountain. Something happened to stop the motor and before anyone could do anything at all, one of the crew threw the anchor into the sea. This made the boat swing round and it was nearly smashed on the rocks, and that's what would have happened if another of the crew hadn't managed to raise the anchor in time.

It wasn't always one of the islanders who fell ill, but sometimes an animal. If an animal fell ill we had to cross to the mainland to fetch the vet. The only one who was available at that time was Mr Thomas from Sarn Mellteyrn and he used to enjoy a trip to Bardsey and of course being paid for going.

'Dammit, the old horse has lost one of its shoes again', we often heard people say on the island. Huw, Ifan's brother, could shoe horses but later Hugh Jones of Gladstone, Aberdaron came to the island to do the shoeing. He was one of the blacksmiths in the village.

In the winter the evenings were very long with no electric light and only candles to provide light. A lot of the women spent the evenings knitting. The man people called Owen Ffatri, from Pen y Caerau, whom I've mentioned before, used to come over to Bardsey regularly and bring sock wool for the women. They used to knit socks in the dark, with the sound of needles clicking against each other.

If the lighthouse needed anything from Aberdaron, the estate would charge them five pounds for using the boat, but generally people would use their own boats and keep the money to help with the costs. The bill for petrol for the engine was paid out of a fund on the island, with each family contributing £2.50 a year, but as Plas Bach was a much bigger farm, they paid £5.

Men used to come to Bardsey to look around the buildings and see if there were any problems anywhere. They used to stay in one of the empty houses while doing the survey. Then finally they went back to their offices and hired other men to come back to Bardsey with the survey report. The men were sent by the owner of the estate, in order to keep all the buildings in excellent condition.

The men who had to do the work spent a long time on the island before completing all the necessary repairs.

When we'd been on Bardsey for some time, the general opinion was that life on Bardsey was no harder at all and though Ifan had been a bit reluctant to come, very soon he realised that we'd made the right decision.

Although the winters were hard and we couldn't cross to the mainland for weeks, we weren't badly off. At one time we went for six weeks without being able to cross the Sound to the mainland to stock up. Food, especially flour, was running short and everybody had emptied their cupboards, and also the lighthouse crew were still helping us out, as always.

In spite of the lack of food there were plenty of potatoes available to make a meal. One other inconvenience which arose when the weather was bad, was that news took a long time to reach the island. Ifan's father died at such a time. We knew nothing of his death or burial until a fortnight after he died. There was no point in lighting a fire on the mountain then, as no-one could cross the Sound in such weather.

Collecting driftwood was very worthwhile as wood was handy for many purposes.

Once, after a storm, I remember a lot of wood coming ashore on Bardsey and Ifan worked really hard collecting the driftwood, as did many of the inhabitants. It was particularly good wood and he made a glass cupboard out of it. Then over to Aberdaron to fetch the glass for it. Once he'd got the glass, everything was ready to finish it off. As he didn't have time then, he took the glass up to one of the bedrooms and put it down on the floor there.

One day soon after, the boat had gone across and a nasty storm had blown up and they couldn't manage to land in the Anchorage as the tides and the wind were against them, and they had to try to bring the boat safely to land in Porth Solfach.

I was in the bedroom watching the boat, and as the sea was so wild, we could only see the boat from time to time. I was afraid I would never see any of the crew alive again. As I watched the boat a woman came into the house and I invited her to the bedroom. She came up to the bedroom and walked on the glass in her heavy clogs and broke it into fragments. That meant another trip to Aberdaron to fetch more glass.

We children all had to be taught a verse from the Bible ready for every Sunday, and there was a prize for the one who learned most verses in a set period. The prize was a certificate stating the fact that so-and-so had excelled in learning verses. Then John Thomas the carpenter would make a neat frame from the Certificate.

It was a great day in the village of Aberdaron when the boat from Bardsey was due, with everyone looking towards Pen y Cil, trying to be first to see the boat rounding the headland. The men on the beach knew exactly when the boat would come into sight.

These were men who had lived by the sea in Aberdaron and knew the movements of the tides inside out. Once the boat had been seen, the telescope would come off the mantelpiece to give them a better view of the boat.

It's not surprising that the boat rounded Trwyn y Pen quickly. There were six or eight muscular men on the oars pulling through the tide. It was wide and heavy, that double-bowed old boat which the people of Bardsey used to carry goods to and from the island. If the wind was favourable, it would help them by filling the sails, two sails on two masts generally.

A lot of men had fairly small boats, and they saw that others had a fairly large boat with double bows. This boat had been made with the two ends identical, so there was no need to turn the boat round on the beach. Rev. Tom Nefyn's father wrote a poem about the boat and here is part of it:

The place where I grew up
You'll find in Aberdaron.
My most vivid memory there
Is father's boat, the 'Salmon'.
That boat the wildest waves could rend,
She had a bow at either end.

You'd see her as she sailed
To Bardsey with her crew;
A wave came from astern,
She'd cut it clean in two.
Her stern the greatest wave had riven,
Her bow had reached the sheltered haven.

Our Bardsey people all
Admired my father's boat
And wondered, could there be
Another such afloat,
Whose planks all weathers could withstand
Thanks to her bow at either end.

I wonder, was this old boat used to carry the tools for building the houses which stand on Bardsey today?

As there was talk of the school closing and as William's health wasn't good, we decided to leave Bardsey Island and return to the mainland once more. It made my heart bleed to leave the island of the Saints and also to leave such a close-knit community. I had tears in my eyes as I shut the door of Carreg Fawr for the last time and believe you me, I often had a quiet little cry over the next few months.

Only once did I return to the island and that was many years later. The place had changed enormously and the houses were empty. Returning to the island brought back many memories to me. I still look back to the old days with deep longing in my heart.

Part XIII

LOOKING BACK

Although it was hard to leave Bardsey, we had to look for a farm on the mainland, and we decided to move to Trefaes Isaf, a farm which was available for rent. Very soon after moving there we made a lot of new friends. The farm is near the village of Sarn Mellteyrn in Llŷn.

After renting it for several years we managed to scrape together enough to buy the farm. Although we were bitterly homesick for Bardsey at times, we had to carry on working hard and bringing up the children. We'd brought the old sheepdog with us from Bardsey but she died within a fortnight. The change was too much for her, more than likely. She wouldn't eat anything and she howled and whined all the time.

It isn't easy to set down all that happened to us on the farm. Like every other family, we had our happy moments, as well as the sad events that come in the course of life, especially when the Second World War came.

Wil joined the army and was sent to the Far East for three years. During that period one of the evacuees came to live with us, a girl the same age as Bessie and to this day she still keeps in touch with us.

On her fifteenth birthday Bessie went to work in Manchester. When Wil returned from the war he went to work with an egg company. People in Llŷn still refer to him as 'Wil wya' (*Will the Eggs*).

Ifor stayed at home for a while, but he wasn't keen on farming and he went to work on the dam at Llanidloes, Powys.

Wil married a girl called Kit Cae Du from Rhoshirwaun. After living for a while in a council house in Botwnnog, they built a bungalow there. Before his death Wil was the manager of Pen y Berth caravan park near Pwllheli and Kit was head cook at Botwnnog Secondary School before retiring in 1995. Their two boys, Kenneth and Gareth, are both married and have families of their own.

Bessie married a boy from Edern, Tom Pentrellech. They farmed in Penrallt and Tŷ Hir, Tudweiliog. They had a son and a daughter, Dafydd and Glenys. Very sadly, Glenys and Tom passed away within three months of each other. Glenys was married and had one daughter, Karen, who lives in Nefyn with her father. She is now nineteen and at Lancaster University.

Bessie and David (who is single) live in a bungalow in Tudweiliog. Ifor married Mary from Lawr y Glyn, Llanidloes, where they live now. Ifor works for a lorry firm and Meri with the Laura Ashley company. They have one son, Robat, who is single.

When Ifan's health broke down, we had to sell the farm and buy a house in Mynytho, 2 St Tudwal's View. It was a fairly big house with a little bungalow behind it, where we two lived, letting out the big house to visitors. But after a while the work of looking after the two places became too much for us and we decided to build a little bungalow. Ifan was ninety-two when he died in 1994 and I will be ninety-one on April 16th 1996. We had been married for sixty-seven happy years.

Before Ifan, Wil and Glenys passed away, there were four generations of girls and four generations of boys in the family. From the early days in Bardsey I am the only survivor. Meri, Tom and Danial have all passed away.

POETRY

I honestly believe that the experience of living among the islanders on Bardsey enriched our lives. It was a community which lived together and worked together in harmony, everyone respecting everyone else.

This is how Bessie, my daughter, set down the experience of her parents who had lived and worked hard to make both ends meet. Here is a poem she wrote to her father and mother to thank them for the way they looked after her.

> The debt I owe my parents
> Is boundless, I believe.
> For every misdemeanour
> Full pardon we received.
>
> I had no life of luxury,
> No worldly wealth at all,
> But loving care and strength were there
> Whatever might befall.
>
> Maybe the ancient saintly souls
> In Bardsey laid to rest
> Burrowed a path up through the soil
> And settled in your breast?
>
> Or did the charm of Bardsey,
> Where breakers never cease,
> Plant love within your bosom
> And fill your heart with peace?
>
> I know that tears fall sometimes
> And hiraeth has its hour
> When I recall that Paradise
> Our old home, Carreg Fawr.

Part XIV

FOOTNOTE

Having spent several months noting down the story of life on Bardsey and my father and mother's experiences on the island at the start of the century I, Bessie, have derived endless enjoyment from setting down the facts, the happy and sad memories which are part of everybody's life story at some point.

Their varied experiences obviously shed light on many aspects of life, earthly and spiritual, which in the end enrich one's journey through life.

I hope that readers will find the book an eye-opener, and that they will perhaps compare their lives with ours. I thank my mother and father for their care and warm love all through my life. My parents were always exceptionally active and their mind and memory crystal clear. Since my father died, mother lives alone in her little bungalow and is coping very well.

I myself am not able to experience the happiness of celebrating fifty years of married life, as I have lost my partner.

I would like to include at this point the following verses which Dafydd, my son, wrote when my father and mother had a special occasion to celebrate:

> To celebrate Granny and Grandpa's fiftieth wedding anniversary:

In nineteen hundred and twenty five
In wedlock two were bound
In the church in Aberdaron
Far from the city's sound.
Ifan Williams Gorlan
And Elen Carreg Fawr
Were united in a marriage
That's lasted to this hour.

I feel sure that you, dear Ifan,
Were bathed in beads of sweat
When on her pretty finger
The wedding ring you set.
And Elen, girl from Bardsey,
Were you completely sure
That this one was the man to be
Your true love evermore?

And you were blessed with children
In Bardsey across the water,
With loving care you brought up
Your two sons and your daughter.
Storms, weeping and rejoicing
Were all part of your world
And you two stayed together
As fifty years unfurled.

This evening in Llanbedrog
Rejoicing here, we too
Your golden wedding feast
Are glad to share with you.
But here tonight your memories
Slip back through time once more
To Tudweiliog, Bardsey and Trefaes
And the church beside the shore.

> I hope, my dear grandparents,
> That you two will enjoy
> Many more years together,
> In blessed peace and joy.

We were also able to enjoy a buffet at home together when my parents celebrated their diamond wedding.

THE FUTURE

Even though I only spent six years on Bardsey, I am thankful for that time, and I honestly believe that most of those who lived on the island feel that the place had an enchantment which cannot be explained. Certainly that is how I feel.

While pondering over the notes for several months, many questions have arisen in my mind about Bardsey.

Will anyone in a hundred years' time be telling our life story?

Will there still be people living on the enchanted island?

Will religion be important there? Will people go there on pilgrimage?

Yes indeed, the future is very unclear for all of us.

A Glossary of Welsh Names

Abaty	Abbey
Aber	River-mouth
Ardal	District
Bach	Small
Bangor	Consecretal land, Monastery
Bedd	Grave
Betws	Prayer house, Chapel
Blaenau	Upland
Bod	Abode
Bryn	Hill
Bwlch	Pass
Bychan	Small
Caban	Hut
Cader	Seat, Stronghold
Cantref	District, Hundred
Caer	Fort, Camp
Capel	Chapel
Castell	Castle
Cefn	Ridge
Celli	Grove
Clas	Mother Church
Coch	Red
Craig	Crag
Crib	Summit
Crwth	Fiddle
Cwm	Valley
Cymru	Wales
Cymry	The Welsh
Din	Hillfort
Dinas	Hillfort, Town
Drwg	Bad, Evil
Du	Black
Dŵr	Water
Dyffryn	Valley
Eglwys	Church
Esgob	Bishop
Ffin	Boundary
Ffordd	Road
Ffridd	Sheepwalk, high pasture
Ffynnon	Well, Spring
Glan	Riverbank
Glas	Green, Blue
Glyn	Glen, Valley
Gwaun	Upland bog
Gwely	Bed, hence family Settlement
Gwlad	Country
Gwyn	White, fair
Hafod	Summer dwelling
Hen	Old
Hendref	Old Township, Winter Settlement
Heol, Hewl	Road
Is	Below
Llan	Church, Place
Llanerch	Glade
Llech	Stone, Rock
Llyn	Lake
Llys	Palace Princes dwelling
Maen	Stone
Maes	Open Field
Mawr	Big, great
Melin	Mill
Moel	Bare hill
Morfa	Marsh, Seashore
Myn	Ore, Mine
Mynachlog	Monastery
Mynydd	Mountain
Nant	Stream, Vale
Newydd	New
Nos	Night
Pandy	Fulling Mill
Pant	Hollow Valley
Parc	Park
Pen	Head, End
Pentref	Hamlet, End Settlement
Perfedd	Middle
Plas	Hall, Mansion
Plwyf	Parish
Pont	Bridge
Porth	Port
Pwll	Pool

Pistyll	Waterfall
Rhaeadr	Waterfall
Rhaglaw	Government Officer
Rhiw	Hill
Rhos	Moor
Rhyd	Ford
Rhyngyll	Beadle
Sarn	Causeway
Sir	Shire
Tir	Land, Territory
Traeth	Beach, shore, stand
Traws	Cross, District
Tref	Township, Town
Tŷ	House
Ty'n Llan	Vicarage, Rectory
Uchaf	Upper
Ynys	Island
Ysbyty	Hospital
Ystad	Estate